ROUTLEDGE LIBRARY EDITIONS:
THE AUTOMOBILE INDUSTRY

Volume 2

STRATEGIC ADJUSTMENT OF PRICE BY JAPANESE AND AMERICAN AUTOMOBILE MANUFACTURERS

STRATEGIC ADJUSTMENT OF PRICE BY JAPANESE AND AMERICAN AUTOMOBILE MANUFACTURERS

KAYE G. HUSBANDS

Routledge
Taylor & Francis Group

LONDON AND NEW YORK

First published in 1993 by Garland Publishing, Inc.

This edition first published in 2018
by Routledge
2 Park Square, Milton Park, Abingdon, Oxon OX14 4RN

and by Routledge
711 Third Avenue, New York, NY 10017

Routledge is an imprint of the Taylor & Francis Group, an informa business

British Library Cataloguing in Publication Data
A catalogue record for this book is available from the British Library

ISBN: 978-1-138-73855-3 (Set)
ISBN: 978-1-315-16182-2 (Set) (ebk)
ISBN: 978-1-138-06317-4 (Volume 2) (hbk)
ISBN: 978-1-315-16119-8 (Volume 2) (ebk)

Publisher's Note
The publisher has gone to great lengths to ensure the quality of this reprint but points out that some imperfections in the original copies may be apparent.

Disclaimer
The publisher has made every effort to trace copyright holders and would welcome correspondence from those they have been unable to trace.

Strategic Adjustment of Price by Japanese and American Automobile Manufacturers

Kaye G. Husbands

Garland Publishing, Inc.
New York & London
1993

Library of Congress Cataloging-in-Publication Data

Husbands, Kaye G., 1959-
    Strategic adjustment of price by Japanese and American automobile
manufacturers / Kaye G. Husbands.
        p.   cm. — (Government and the economy : outstanding studies and
recent dissertations)
    Originally presented as the author's thesis (Harvard University).
    Includes bibliographical references and index.
    ISBN 0-8153-1228-8 (alk. paper)
    1. Automobiles—Prices—Japan—Econometric models. 2. Automobiles—
Prices—United States—Econometric models. I. Title. II. Series: Government and
the economy.
HD9710.J32H87   1993
338.4'36292'0952—dc20   92-35293
                                                                  CIP

Printed on acid-free, 250-year-life paper
Manufactured in the United States of America

To my parents:
Waple V. Husbands
Humphrey O. Husbands

Contents

Tables and Figures

TABLE

FIGURE

Preface

U.S. automobile producers believed that the Japanese-U.S. Voluntary Export Restraint (VER) would impede Japanese penetration of the domestic small car market and bolster their competitive strength in domestic and world markets. With the purpose of investigating whether or not such expectations were realized, this study develops for the domestic automobile industry a demand-supply model which is used to determine the VER's effects on market behavior and national welfare. Specifically, the following questions are addressed: (1) What was the VER's effect on pricing strategies of U.S. and Japanese manufacturers in the domestic car market? (2) Did U.S. manufacturers capture market share while the VER was in effect? (3) Who benefitted from the VER--Japanese or U.S. manufacturers, domestic dealers of Japanese or U.S. cars, domestic consumers?

The following chapters develop the framework for and present the results of an econometric simulation of the transaction and wholesale prices, quantities demanded and produced, manufacturer's costs and factor demands. Estimates of demand elasticities, marginal costs and conjectural variation parameters (which reveal pricing strategies) are outputs of model estimation. The VER's impact on profits and consumer welfare are generated from the simulation results.

This dissertation was completed a Harvard University under the supervision of Prof. Richard E. Caves and Prof. Hendrik Houthakker. AT&T Bell Laboratories provided the funding for all of my graduate work.

K.G.H.

Acknowledgments

Throughout the many phases of this dissertation, I have been encouraged and supported by faculty advisors, organizations, friends and relatives. I am grateful to all who assisted me, with special thanks to those listed below.

Richard E. Caves has played a key role in my development as an economist. Professor Caves inspired me to pursue the fields of Industrial Organization and International Trade, promoted my willingness to tackle a challenging dissertation topic and faithfully guided my academic endeavors.

Hendrik Houthakker shared with me invaluable perspectives in the process of developing my empirical model. Professor Houthakker provided assistance in the structure and use of my data set. In addition, he helped me fine-tune the model and increase its performance.

Kala Krishna's theoretical analysis of the VER was the inspiration for this empirical study. I am also grateful that she served as third reader on my dissertation defense committee. Professor Krishna's instructive comments greatly encouraged me and are bases for my future research in this area.

Anna Aizcorbe, Data Resources, Inc. and U.S. Department of Labor, Bureau of Labor Statistics generously supplied data for this study. The accuracy of such data greatly enhanced the quality of my results.

AT&T Bell Laboratories financed my graduate education through its Cooperative Research Fellowship Program. Through this program, I worked with Robert Dansby, my designated mentor, and drew from his knowledge of economics. Dr. Dansby challenged me to excel and often advocated on my behalf with his colleagues. Harvard University and Williams College also provided tangible support for this study.

My close friends Kimberly Hawkins and Carolyn Brown proofread various drafts of this work, helped gather and enter reams of data and consistently supported my efforts to complete this dissertation.

Their friendship provided balance and perspective which enabled me to persevere.

I extend my deepest appreciation to my parents. Their encouraging words and self-sacrifice have sustained me throughout the years. The successful completion of this dissertation is attributable in large part to their diligent example, unfailing love and inspiring vision. Special thanks to my father for being a sounding board for my ideas along the way and for proofreading this document.

Above all, I thank the Lord God for giving purpose and direction to my life and for providing supportive and encouraging relationships which I shall treasure always.

Strategic Adjustment of Price by Japanese and American Automobile Manufacturers

1.0 Introduction

In March 1981, the Japanese government agreed to U.S. demands for limits on the exports of Japanese passenger cars to the United States.[1] Domestically, proponents embraced the Japanese-U.S. Voluntary Export Restraint (VER) as a policy instrument which would stabilize profits and employment in the automobile industry. U.S. automobile producers perceived the VER as a means by which Japanese penetration of the then growing domestic small car market would be impeded. They also anticipated that strategic investment of revenues earned as a result of the VER would facilitate their efforts to gain a strong competitive position in domestic and world markets.

U.S producers' expectations of significant gains from the imposition of the VER had some merit. For international trade theory predicts that in oligopolistic industries--such as the automobile industry--equilibrium prices and profits of foreign and domestic firms will be higher under a VER than under free trade. However, quantities sold of the domestic firms may increase or decrease with a VER, depending on the values of own- and cross-price elasticities of demand. Thus, it is possible for national welfare to increase only if domestic quantities are increased, average price-cost margins of domestic firms are sufficiently large and gains to foreign firms are sufficiently small. But some economists see the more likely result of the VER would be

---

[1]The VER is sometimes referred to in the literature as the Voluntary Restraint Agreement (VRA). Beginning April 1, 1981, the Japanese announced their first quantity limits on car exports to be 1.68 million for the year ending March 31, 1982. The initial agreement stated that the VER would be in effect for the following two, possibly three years, but with upward adjustments to be made according to increases in domestic sales of U.S. cars. The Japanese have continued to announce their export limits and have set restraints for their fiscal year beginning April 1989 at 2.3 million.

to show the losses of domestic consumers exceeding the gains of domestic producers and, therefore, a decline in the national welfare. (See Krishna, 1983/84; Harris, 1984; Itoh and Ono,1984; Ono,1984).

The VER's effect on equilibrium prices and quantities and thus on consumer and producer surplus is, in part, the result of its influence on competition in the targeted industry. Krishna (1984) shows that a VER set at or slightly below the free trade level creates a more collusive market. Specifically, by assuming that a Bertrand-Nash equilibrium exists during free trade and that the domestic and foreign goods are close substitutes, Krishna shows that the profit functions and hence the price reaction functions of representative foreign and domestic firms are altered by the existence of a VER.[2]

Under these conditions, an equilibrium in pure strategies is no longer attainable. The new equilibrium is instead a mixed strategy equilibrium where the foreign firm sets a single price and the domestic firm randomizes over its set of profit maximizing prices in selecting its market price. Both firms earn higher profits, with the domestic

---

[2]These results also hinge on the following assumptions. The industry has one domestic and one foreign firm that strategically set prices to maximize profits earned in the domestic market. The industry's product is heterogeneous and domestic consumers perceive the variants of the product as imperfect substitutes. Rationing of the foreign good affects demand for the domestic good. There exists a numeraire good and thus income effects are assumed away. The Nash equilibrium concept is imposed and the reaction functions and the market equilibrium satisfy existence, uniqueness and stability conditions with and without the VER. The VER is set at or close to the free trade level.

manufacturer earning the profits of a price leader.[3] Thus, the presence of a VER can effect a change in the manufacturers' behavior.

The theory explains why higher prices accompany VERs and why foreign manufacturers favor VERs over other forms of trade restraints. However, the theory is limited in three ways. First, without estimates of demand elasticities, it cannot unambiguously predict the VER's impact on quantities demanded of the domestic good or on national welfare. Second, it cannot predict the magnitudes by which prices or profits increase, or the magnitude of losses to consumers during a VER regime. Third, the assumed state of market behavior in the pre-VER period in part determines the expected behavioral outcome as well as the equilibrium prices and quantities under the VER. Thus, if the rivalry among automobile producers does not coincide with that posited by the theory, the theoretical model becomes an inadequate predictor of the VER effects for that industry. Empirical models are, therefore, used in this thesis to examine such issues.

Previous empirical studies of the restraints' impact on the automobile industry all agree with the theoretical predictions that the VER hurts purchasers of automobiles and benefits both domestic and Japanese automobile manufacturers (see Feenstra (1984); Gomez-Ibanez, Leone and O'Connell (1983); Crandall (1984,1985); Tarr and Morkre (1984); Hickok (1985); Mannering and Winston (1987); Collyns and Dunaway (1987); Willig and Dutz (1987); Dinopoulos and Kreinin (1988)). All of these studies also find that average prices of domestic and foreign makes would have been lower

---

[3]Harris (1984) also assumes that firms exhibit Bertrand-Nash behavior before the VER is imposed. He derives similar results to Krishna's. However, he considers only the set of prices for which the VER is binding and therefore derives an equilibrium in pure strategies where the domestic firm *becomes* the price leader under the VER regime. In Krishna (1983) there is also a case where it is assumed that the domestic firm is a Stackelberg leader and specific demand functions are introduced. The equilibrium in pure strategies exists and is unique with or without the VER. In this case the qualitative results reported above hold for both prices and profits. Domestic outputs are shown to decrease because of the specified numerical values of slopes of the demand curves.

had the VER not been imposed. Not surprisingly, there is no consensus about the restriction's effect on quantities sold of domestically produced cars. Some researchers estimate that fewer domestic makes would have been sold without the VER, while others reach the opposite conclusion. This ambiguity in the overall findings could stem from the differences in methodologies applied as well as from the nonuniform nature of the data.

Although these empirical studies verify the theoretical predictions of Krishna and Harris referred to above, none has attempted to answer the following two important questions regarding the effects of the VER on pricing strategies and profits: (1) How was the nature of competition in the domestic car market affected by the VER? (2) How much of the profits (or losses) generated by domestic sales of Japanese cars accrued to domestic dealers and thus should be entered as an adjustment to U.S. national welfare?

Therefore, the purpose of this study is to develop for the domestic automobile industry a demand-supply model which incorporates both wholesale and retail sectors, and which allows strategic pricing behavior of U.S. and Japanese producers to be endogenously determined. It is assumed that similarities in technologies permit the aggregation of manufacturers in which the parent firm is located. Thus the analysis proceeds as though there were only two firms, U.S. and Japanese. The cars sold by U.S. producers are categorized as either small or large, while those sold by Japanese producers are categorized only as small cars.

A time series approach is used. The pre-VER period runs from the first quarter of 1973 to the first quarter of 1981, while the VER period runs from the second quarter of 1981 to the fourth quarter of 1986. The model is estimated for the entire period 1973:1 to 1986:4 and a simulation of the model is used to forecast retail (transaction) prices, wholesale prices and quantities for the VER period. These predicted values are assumed to be those which would have prevailed had the restraints not been imposed. They are used together with the actual values of these variables to calculate the VER's impact on prices, quantities and profits of both manufacturers and dealers. In essence, it has been assumed that the VER was the predominant factor which did not exist during the historical period and which influenced market equilibrium during the VER regime.

The degree to which consumers perceive Japanese cars and U.S. cars as substitutes should be reflected in the model's estimates of price flexibility[4] and of demand elasticities. These estimated elasticities are expected to indicate that Japanese cars were better substitutes for U.S. small cars than for U.S. large cars. The type of market behavior which existed before and during the VER should be reflected in the model's estimates of conjectural variations (CV) parameters. Although U.S. manufacturers are the dominant producers in the domestic market in terms of market share, Japanese producers are expected to be the price leaders in the small car market. No prior expectation is made with respect to the U.S. large car price response to a change in Japanese car prices. Comparison of the CV parameter estimates for the pre-VER and VER periods is expected to reveal a movement toward U.S. price leadership in the small car market as quantity restraints on Japanese cars prevent the Japanese from maintaining their leadership role. The consistency of the estimated conjectural variation parameters with actual market behavior is statistically tested.

For both Japanese and U.S. cars, the model's simulation of the 1980's domestic market without the influence of the VER is expected to yield lower retail and wholesale price than those which existed under the VER. There is no *ex ante* prediction, however, of the VER's effect on quantities sold of U.S. cars or of its effects on profits earned by producers and domestic dealers. This is because these outcomes depend heavily on the model's estimates of the demand slopes and of the conjectural variation parameters.

In Chapter 2 of this thesis, the previous empirical models which focused on assessing the VER's impact on profitability in the domestic automobile market are reviewed. Two methodologies are distinguished among those models: those which rely on base-year data to predict either the VER or the non-VER equilibrium prices and quantities for the 1980's, and those which use the *ex post* forecasting method to predict the non-VER equilibrium prices for comparison to actual prices for the 1980's. The advantages and limitations of the two methodologies as well as specific assumptions and procedures used in the previous empirical models are discussed. The outcome of this critical review suggests the use of the *ex post* forecasting method for the present analysis and highlights the necessary innovations for

---

[4]The responsiveness of price to a change in quantity.

obtaining more accurate estimates of the VER's effects on domestic welfare.

Chapter 3 describes the demand-supply model which is developed for the current analysis. Since one purpose of this study is the assessment of the VER's effects on profits of both dealers and manufacturers, the model includes consumer demand and dealer demand equations. These equations are used in simulation to predict transaction prices and quantities. To facilitate the estimation of the type of market behavior during the pre-VER and VER periods, manufacturer behavioral equations are also included in the model. These equations enable the model to estimate the CV parameters as well as to simulate wholesale prices without the VER. Since the manufacturer behavioral equations require estimates of marginal cost in order to identify the CV parameters, cost equations are included in the model. Input demand equations supply the necessary cross equation restrictions on the cost parameters. Marginal costs of Japanese and U.S. automobile manufacturers are thus analytically derived from the cost equations and are substituted into their respective manufacturer behavioral equations for estimation within the simultaneous system. These estimates of marginal costs are used in the determination of the VER's effects on manufacturer profits.

The availability of data and methods used to convert the raw data into the required time series are described in Chapter 4. Aggregate time series data on transaction prices, wholesale prices and quantities were constructed from model or segment specific data. The procedures used to convert firm specific data on production costs to aggregates for Japanese and U.S. producers are also given in detail. The sources of these and other data such as demand shift variables and price deflators are also disclosed.

In Chapter 5, the results of the analysis are presented and compared to selected results of previous studies. Of all the findings, the most significant and, possibly, surprising are:

1. Japanese price leadership *vis-à-vis* U.S. small and large cars cannot be rejected for the pre-VER period.

2. There is evidence of movement toward Bertrand pricing or toward U.S. price leadership with the VER.

3. U.S. manufacturers actually sold fewer cars under the VER than they would have sold had the VER not been imposed.

4. U.S. automobile manufacturers and domestic automobile dealers win, while Japanese automobile manufacturers and domestic automobile consumers lose because of the VER, dealers gaining more than manufacturers. The total U.S. welfare effect is positive.

Estimates of price flexibility, of demand and of gasoline price elasticities are also presented in this Chapter.

Concluding remarks and suggestions for future research are set forth in Chapter 6. The Appendices contain regression results as well as lists of the automobiles used in creating the quantity, wholesale price and transaction price series.

2.0 Previous Studies

2.1 OVERVIEW

This Chapter presents a historical review of empirical studies on the Japanese-U.S. VER and discusses the merits and limitations of the methodologies which have been used to study the VER's efficacy. In keeping with the present analysis, only those studies which evaluate the VER's effects on the profitability of firms in the domestic automobile market are reviewed. Studies which primarily assess the VER's impact on consumer welfare or on product quality are therefore excluded from the discussion.[5]

The studies reviewed can be placed in one of two methodological categories:

(1) base-year simulation method [Gomez-Ibanez, Leone and O'Connell (1983), Tarr and Morkre (1984)], or

(2) *ex post* forecast method [Willig and Dutz (1987), Crandall (1985), Mannering and Winston (1987), Collyns and Dunaway (1987)].

The latter technique is distinguished from the former in that actual changes in the economic conditions of the market are reflected in the simulated values for the forecast period.

Sections 2.2 and 2.3, respectively, provide a critical examination of each methodology. Each section also contains a critique of the individual models. This is accomplished, wherever possible, by comparing and contrasting parallel procedures peculiar to those studies

---

[5]Those aspects of the studies selected for review which deal with consumer welfare or product quality are also omitted from the discussion.

which share the same general methodology. Section 2.4 gives summary remarks.

2.2 BASE-YEAR SIMULATION METHOD (BYSM)

BYSM is a comparative statics exercise in which the base year solutions to a system of equations is compared to other particular solutions of the same system which are generated under alternative economic scenarios. Since predetermined values of the model's coefficients can be used and since actual values for the simulated period are not required, this method is less data-intensive than its alternative, the forecast method. Apparently, this attribute appealed to early analysts of the VER's effects because actual data was unavailable for much of the period under examination. BYSM, however, has two drawbacks, both of which stem from its limited use of data. First, projections of the VER's effects are not very reliable if market conditions for the simulated period diverge from those in the base year. Second, the procedure requires extensive use of results which are determined outside the model.

Gomez-Ibanez et. al. and Tarr and Morkre both use BYSM, but they take opposite approaches to analyze the VER effects in their models. While the former authors observe the change in market equilibrium precipitated by the imposition of the VER, the others consider the effects of having the VER removed. Unlike Gomez-Ibanez et. al., Tarr and Morkre are unable to forecast all of their endogenous variables within their demand-supply system. Therefore, without the VER, they estimate the Japanese price for 1981 by adjusting its 1980 value for increases in factor prices, for appreciation of the yen against the dollar, and for an upward shift in product mix, all of which occurred during the two years.[6] This price is then used to generate

---

[6]In an effort to avoid underestimating the VER's effects on consumer welfare, Tarr and Morkre implicitly attribute the entire change in product quality to the VER. Since part of the VER's impact on profits comes from these quality effects, this adjustment contributes to their underestimation of the VER's effect on profits earned by the Japanese and possibly on profits earned by U.S. producers.

estimates of the other endogenous variables which would have prevailed had the VER not been implemented.

Closer examination of the two models reveals not only similarities in the way demand equations were developed, but also differences in the assumptions pertaining to supply relationships, market behavior and equilibrium conditions. Specifically, Gomez-Ibanez et. al. as well as Tarr and Morkre specify systems of demand equations in which the interdependence of demand for Japanese and U.S. cars is taken into account. Unlike Tarr and Morkre, however, the former authors construct a multi-product demand system which is based on Deaton and Muellbauer's (1980a) Almost Ideal Demand System.[7] Within this framework, they explain demands by relative prices and total real expenditure, thereby omitting other demand shift variables from their equations.[8] Additionally, unlike Tarr and Morkre, Gomez-Ibanez et. al. assume that there is a representative consumer in the market who divides his budget between cars and a composite

---

[7]The structure of the Almost Ideal Demand System allows for exact non-linear aggregation over consumers and is consistent with constrained consumer utility maximization. The first characteristic allows the authors exogenously to specify more independent restrictions than if they had used a system which imposes linear Engel curves such as the Linear Expenditure System. The authors use the second characteristic to impose homogeneity and Slutsky symmetry restrictions on their price and income elasticity estimates. Since market shares are estimated, the adding-up restriction is automatically satisfied.

[8]Deaton and Muellbauer originally developed their system of demand to examine the demand for non-durable goods. They do not include demand shift variables other than expenditures in their Engel curve equations for two reasons. First, consumer theory predicts that demand for goods which do not affect the wealth of a representative consumer is adequately explained by relative prices and total real expenditure. Second, it is a source of debate whether demand shift variables should enter the consumer's utility function, the consumer's budget constraint, or both. Thus a strict adoption of the Deaton and Muellbauer structure is not sufficient to explain demand for durable goods such as automobiles.

commodity. They categorize all domestically sold cars as either basic small cars, luxury small cars, or traditional cars. American cars are represented in all three market segments while Japanese cars are represented in only the first two. European cars are grouped with American cars since European producers are assumed to share with U.S. manufacturers in any volume increases under the VER. Gomez-Ibanez et. al. further assume that the consumer perceives American and Japanese cars in the same segment as closer substitutes than those in different segments. The demand system therefore has six equations: one for each of the five car types and one for the composite commodity.

There are further differences between the two approaches. Tarr and Morkre adopt a more simple, two-equation demand system. Only demands for Japanese and American cars are identified. European cars are omitted from their analysis because they assume independence of demand for Japanese and American cars from the price of European cars. Indeed, quantities are determined only by the prices of Japanese and American cars. Income and other demand shift variables are omitted from their demand equations.

Both studies omit variables from their demand equations which have been shown by previous studies to explain demand for automobiles. Since neither study uses econometric procedures to estimate the demand elasticities, the omissions affect only the intercepts of the equations and not the coefficients of the included explanatory variables. However, the omissions impair the ability of the authors to predict the VER's effects for market conditions other than those present during the base year.

Gomez-Ibanez et. al. compensate for this limitation of their model by estimating the VER's effects under two different assumptions about the strength of the domestic market. In one case, it is assumed that the demand for automobiles is depressed to an annual value of 8.8 million cars, similar to that which existed from 1980 through 1982. Under this scenario, the VER is assumed to be set at 1.68 million. In the other case, market demand is assumed to be stronger, with total demand for automobiles set at 11.5 million cars and the VER set at 2.13 million. The authors expected this more buoyant market for automobiles to prevail in 1983.

In contrast, Tarr and Morkre do not compensate for exogenous changes in the automobile market other than for the VER. They only consider the effects of removing a VER under market conditions which prevailed during 1981. They do, however, use their estimates to evaluate the VER's welfare effects up to six years after its implementation. Since 1981 was a weak year for automobile sales, Tarr and Morkre admit that they underestimate the VER's effects for those years in which the domestic demand for automobiles was stronger than it was in 1981. It should also be noted that since they select 1981 as their base year, it may be fair to argue that they implicitly assume that the VER was the sole reason for the difference between their simulated values and the actual values for that year. By contrast, Gomez-Ibanez et. al. are not compelled to make this assumption to carry out their analysis since they do not use actual data pertaining to the VER period.

Both studies calibrate demand elasticities to coincide with those estimated by earlier automobile demand studies. Gomez-Ibanez et. al. use the properties of their theoretically consistent demand system (i.e., adding-up, symmetry and homogeneity) to estimate own- and cross-price elasticities for each defined market segment. They utilize the degrees of freedom inherent in the system to specify half of the price and income elasticities and to impose the cross-equation restrictions on the elasticities. The model is calibrated to have an industry demand elasticity of unity, with individual market segment elasticities deviating from unity according to industry rules-of-thumb. For example, the own-price elasticity for American luxury cars are assumed to be slightly smaller in absolute value than those for American basic cars (2.25 and 3.25, respectively). The system is also required to approximate 1980 prices and quantities under the weak market scenario.

Assuming Slutsky symmetry conditions hold, Tarr and Morkre calibrate their own- and cross-price elasticities to be consistent with the results of Toder's (1978) study. Toder estimates that the percentage change in the share of Japanese cars to domestically sold U.S. cars caused by a one percent change in the relative price of Japanese cars to that of U.S. cars (i.e., elasticity of substitution) is -2. However, in order to convert this elasticity into individual coefficients for the demand equations, the authors use the findings of previous studies which indicate that the overall demand elasticity is -1. Therefore, Tarr and Morkre and Gomez-Ibanez et. al. use the same benchmark demand elasticity to derive their respective demand coefficients.

The procedures used in both studies to estimate demand elasticities are problematic for two reasons. First, calibrating the elasticities to maintain consistency with previous models presumes that consumer preferences for automobiles were the same in the 1960's and early 1970's as they were in the late 1970's and 1980's. In view of the changes in automobile characteristics over the years, it is unlikely that consumer preferences would have remained the same.[9] Since previous studies only yield average estimates of price and income elasticities for U.S. and Japanese cars, the multi-product elasticities used by Gomez-Ibanez et. al. are based largely on presumption.[10]

The second problem with the demand elasticity estimates is that the introduction of symmetry and (in the case of Gomez-Ibanez et. al.) homogeneity conditions in the demand equations places restrictions on consumer preferences which may not actually exist in the market. In fact, having estimated demand systems for non-durable goods, Deaton and Muellbauer conclude that the properties of homogeneity and symmetry are not inherent in aggregate demand functions. Their finding concurs with that of Barten (1969). Therefore, the method of calibration and the imposition of restrictions applied in both studies call into question the appropriateness and therefore the accuracy of the estimated demand equations used to evaluate the VER effects.

On the supply side, the two studies make different behavioral assumptions. Gomez-Ibanez et. al. assume that, before and after the VER is imposed, Japanese firms maximize joint profits, having perfect knowledge of U.S. price and quantity responses. The strategic responses of U.S. producers to a change in the Japanese price are not limited to those which maximize their profits. Instead, the authors assume that U.S. producers either adjust quantities alone, adjust prices alone, or adjust both quantities and prices in equal proportions. These alternative behavior patterns are consistent with infinite, zero or unitary

---

[9]Tsurumi and Tsurumi (1983) report a shift in domestic consumer preferences away from large cars toward smaller economy cars. This issue is discussed at greater length in Chapter 3 of this thesis.

[10]Gomez-Ibanez et. al. admit that the studies from which they obtain their price elasticity estimates have econometric problems, including failure to differentiate between short- and long-run elasticities, multicollinearity and limited price variation.

supply elasticity, respectively.[11] In effect, Gomez-Ibanez et. al. assume Japanese price leadership.

In contrast, Tarr and Morkre assume that Japanese and U.S. producers price competitively in the domestic market, with or without the VER. They specify a simple linear supply curve for U.S. producers, assuming an elasticity of supply of approximately 10.[12] For Japanese firms, an infinite supply elasticity is assumed to exist without the restraint. When the VER is in effect, Japanese firms are assumed to charge exactly that price which clears the market.

Although both studies maintain different assumptions about the behavior of firms in the domestic automobile market, neither assumes behavioral conditions which are consistent with market studies or with theoretical predictions. Tarr and Morkre assume perfectly competitive behavior exists before and during the VER. Studies by White (1971), Adams (1986) and several other industry analysts show that among U.S. producers, Ford and Chrysler follow General Motors' lead when setting prices. Thus prices are not based purely on marginal costs of production. Gomez-Ibanez et. al. assume Japanese price leadership to prevail before and during the VER. Stated differently, they assume that market behavior is independent of the trade regime. Itoh and Ono (1984), however, show that if firms are following profit maximizing strategies, then it is optimal for the domestic firm to be the price leader in a VER regime.[13] The ability of both models accurately to predict the VER's effects on profits is therefore jeopardized by the inadequacy of their respective behavioral assumptions.

It is difficult to compare the quantitative results of the two models since there are many differences in the types of data used. For

---

[11]From their simulations the authors conclude that the first response is consistent with employment maximization, while the last response is consistent with profit maximization.

[12]Tarr and Morkre derive their estimate from data reported in a study by Charles River Associates (1976).

[13]They assume that there is one home firm and one foreign firm and that the goods are imperfect substitutes. They also prove this result for homogeneous goods in their 1982 paper.

example, Tarr and Morkre use quality adjusted unit values[14] while Gomez-Ibanez use average retail prices. In addition, there is a one year difference in their choices of base years which could account for some difference in the magnitude of their results. Qualitatively, however, the models reach the same conclusions. U.S. quantities as well as prices and profits of both U.S. and Japanese producers increase because of the VER. These results are consistent with the trade theoretic predictions.

In summary, the primary benefit of using BYSM to analyze the VER effects is its relatively small data requirement. However, this benefit is accompanied by the countervailing disadvantages of outdated demand coefficient estimates as well as unreliable long-term forecasts.

2.3 EX POST FORECAST METHOD (EPFM)

EPFM utilizes identified relationships between endogenous variables and predetermined explanatory variables to forecast values of the former under alternative market conditions. Such relationships are usually established through regression techniques, although some studies draw inferences from simple correlative factors. Using this method, the VER's effects are measured by comparing forecasted values to actual values for the period under examination. The overriding assumption, therefore, is that relationships which existed before the VER would have been maintained had there been no market intervention.

As a technique, EPFM improves on BYSM by allowing changes in exogenous market conditions to be reflected in forecasted values. Also, unlike BYSM, EPFM allows the use of more recent estimates of demand and supply equations. These two attributes of EPFM increase the reliability of longer term predictions of the VER's effects.

Among the four studies that apply this technique, that of Willig and Dutz employs the simplest structure, relying heavily on predetermined estimates of market trends, on demand elasticities and on price-cost margins. These authors estimate the effect of the VER on the combined profits of U.S. manufacturers and dealers as follows:

---

[14]Unit values are comparable to wholesale prices.

$$\Pi^{US} = \Delta QD^{US} * (P - MC) * CPIAUTOS,$$

where, Π^{US} denotes the VER-induced change in profits earned by U.S. manufacturers and dealers, ΔQD^{US} denotes the VER-induced change in quantities sold of U.S. cars, P denotes the average price of U.S. cars before the VER, MC denotes the marginal cost of the average U.S. car before the VER, and CPIAUTOS denotes the consumer price index for automobiles sold domestically.

Willig and Dutz calculate ΔQD^{US} by first estimating the degree to which the VER is binding. This is accomplished by employing reported estimates of the Japanese market share and of the pre-VER growth rates of domestic demand for automobiles to extrapolate what domestic sales of Japanese cars would have been in the 1980's without the restraint. They estimate that in 1985, the VER reduced Japanese car imports by approximately 1 million. Using previous estimates of price elasticities of demand, Willig and Dutz determine that every two Japanese cars are replaced by one U.S. car. Applying this substitution factor to the estimated 1 million car reduction of Japanese imports yields a gain of approximately 500,000 in U.S. cars domestically sold in 1985. This increase does not account for the more indirect effects of the VER such as changes in prices stemming from oligopoly power or from adjustments in product mix.

Since there are significant differences among previous estimates of the VER's effects on the price of U.S. cars, Willig and Dutz are reluctant to develop their own-price equation. Their ability to obtain a direct estimate of the VER's impact on U.S. price-cost margins is thereby inhibited. As an alternative, the authors assume that the margins between retail price and marginal costs during the VER period differed from their pre-VER values only by an inflation factor. A weighted average of the price-cost margin for the average U.S. car is therefore calculated from price and cost data reported in Gomez-Ibanez et. al., with an adjustment by CPIAUTOS. The estimate of the price-cost margin for 1985 is approximately $1,840 which, when applied to the change in U.S. quantities, yields an estimated $920 million increase in U.S. profits resulting from the VER in that year.

Willig and Dutz also determine the extent to which increases in prices of Japanese cars during the 1980's reflected the VER's influence. The authors first establish that, prior to the VER, the average unit price of Japanese cars domestically sold was highly correlated with a benchmark index[15] of the marginal costs of producing a Japanese car. They then presume that the relationship would have persisted had the VER not been imposed. Any deviation of the Japanese price from the benchmark is thus assumed to be the result of the VER. Willig and Dutz find that the VER effected a 13% increase in domestic prices of Japanese cars in 1982, 16% in 1983, and over 18% in 1984.[16] The high correlation between the Japanese price and the benchmark index prior to the VER indicates that Japanese manufacturers were competitively pricing among themselves during that period. Since the VER is expected to facilitate collusive pricing behavior among Japanese producers, these estimated price increases are expected to include effects attributable to the existence of oligopoly power in the Japanese automobile industry.

Three problems result from the lack of formally specified demand and price equations in the Willig and Dutz study. First, the authors must rely on demand elasticities which were determined in previous models. The studies from which they select their elasticity estimates are: Gomez-Ibanez et. al. and Tarr and Morkre which, as earlier discussed, also rely on outdated demand elasticity estimates; and Hunker (1983) which uses a procedure similar to Gomez-Ibanez et. al. to estimate demand elasticities. The second problem is that, because the authors have no price equation (or relationship) for the U.S. manufacturers, they rely on an adjustment rule which assumes that the percentage increase in price equalled the percentage increase in costs during the 1980's, whether or not the VER was in place. This rule is

---

[15]The benchmark index is comprised of the dollar-yen exchange rate, Japanese factor prices, changes in product quality and regulatory costs.

[16]Since the benchmark index is adjusted for quality increases, the price increases associated with quality upgrading during the VER are not reflected in these estimates. The authors also utilize previous estimates of own-price elasticities of the demand for Japanese cars domestically sold and their estimate of the degree to which the VER is binding to obtain an estimate of the VER's impact on Japanese prices. This procedure indicates that the VER raised domestic prices of Japanese cars by 10 to 15 percent. Again, this only measures the consumer demand effect.

not based on empirical findings. Also, it is unlikely that the value of the adjustment factor would be the same across trade regimes. Third, in the absence of a simultaneous solution of supply and demand equations, only first round effects of the VER are estimated.

In contrast to Willig and Dutz, Crandall (1985) evaluates the VER's effects on the profits of U.S. and Japanese producers by focusing on the VER's price effects. He first estimates price equations for Japanese and U.S. producers, then compares actual values at the retail level for the VER period to forecasted values generated by his estimated equations. Crandall chooses to estimate the domestic retail price of Japanese cars in two stages. In the first stage, the average unit value of Japanese cars is regressed on factor prices, capacity utilization in the Japanese automobile industry, and the dollar-yen exchange rate. In the second stage, the average retail price of Japanese cars is regressed on the average unit value of Japanese cars and seasonal dummy variables. The unit value and retail price equations are estimated for the period 1976:1 to 1980:4 and then used to predict what Japanese prices would have been for the period 1981:1 to 1984:2 in the absence of the VER. Comparison of actual and predicted values for 1984 reveals that the VER increased Japanese prices by $2,500 (or 40%).[17]

Crandall assumes that U.S. producers consider the retail prices of Japanese cars when setting prices. Since he expects the interdependence of demand for U.S. and Japanese cars to vary by automobile size classes, the U.S. price equation is estimated for a pooled sample for the years 1975 to 1984, with U.S. cars partitioned into four market segments. He assumes that retail prices of U.S. cars are determined by factor prices and capacity utilization in the U.S. automobile industry, compliance costs related to federal emissions and safety regulations, the segment of the market served, and the retail price of Japanese cars. Since all of Crandall's equations are estimated in log-linear form, the coefficient on the Japanese price in the U.S. price equation is a form of conjectural elasticity--the average percentage

---

[17]This estimate does not include adjustments for product quality. If such adjustments are taken into consideration, then the estimate is approximately $2,350. Since the present analysis focuses on the VER's impact on profits and not on consumer welfare, the relevant statistic is the unadjusted value.

change in U.S. list prices in response to a one percent change in the Japanese list prices. Crandall assumes the average conjectural elasticity for all U.S. cars to be 0.4. He estimates the VER's effect on the average list price by multiplying the change in the Japanese list price by the average conjectural elasticity. The estimated effect of the VER on the average U.S. price is $1000 (or 10%) for 1984. Ignoring the VER's effects on quantities sold, Crandall calculates the VER's effect on revenues of Japanese and U.S. producers by multiplying the estimated changes in prices by quantities sold during 1984. He finds that the VER generated a $4.6 billion increase in revenues from domestic sales of Japanese cars and an $8 billion increase in revenues from domestic sales of U.S. cars in that year.[18]

There are two shortcomings in Crandall's analysis of the VER's impact on prices and profitability in the domestic automobile industry. First, by omitting U.S. prices from the Japanese price equation, while including Japanese prices in the U.S. price equations, he has presumed oligopolistic behavior consistent with his assumptions about Japanese price leadership *vis-à-vis* U.S. producers. Surveyed industry studies show no clear indication as to the nature of competition between U.S. and Japanese automobile makers. Although it might be reasonable to believe that such behavior exists in the small car market, there is less reason to expect Japanese price leadership to prevail in other market segments since U.S. producers dominate the markets for larger cars. Furthermore, Crandall estimates a constant conjectural elasticity for a period which includes both the constrained and unconstrained trade regimes. According to trade theoretic models, it is unlikely that behavior would be the same in the two regimes and that the U.S. producers would continue to behave as price followers once the VER is imposed.[19]

A second shortcoming of Crandall's analysis is that he does not estimate demand or cost equations, nor does he utilize previously

---

[18]These estimates assume an average conjectural elasticity of 0.4.

[19]See Krishna (1984) and Itoh and Ono (1984). Also, in the light of the research by Willig and Dutz (1987), it is unlikely that the relationship between the Japanese price and dollar-yen exchange rate remained constant between the two regimes.

determined estimates of price elasticities or marginal costs. His estimate of the VER's impact on profits relies solely on the estimated price increases. It is clear that more accurate estimates of the welfare effects of the VER associated with gains (or losses) to producers and domestic dealers would be obtained if these other effects had been measured.

To estimate the VER's impact on the market equilibrium, Mannering and Winston (1987) utilize Crandall's estimates of the VER's price effects, an estimated cost function developed by Aizcorbe, Winston and Friedlaender (1987), and their own vehicle demand forecasting system.[20] On the demand side, vehicle prices and characteristics, consumer characteristics and consumer vehicle experiences are the determining factors in a household's vehicle purchase decision. Market demand for a particular new or used vehicle is determined by adding up the number of households which are likely to purchase the vehicle. On the supply side, quantities produced of U.S., Japanese or other imported cars are determined by vehicle prices and characteristics. Supplies are assumed to be perfectly elastic with respect to price. In equilibrium, prices are such that quantities demanded for new and used vehicles and the numbers of scrapped vehicles equal quantities of new and used vehicles produced.

Although equilibrium prices are determined within the system, the reduced form price equations are not specified. Therefore, Mannering and Winston determine the VER's effects on equilibrium quantities by priming their system with Crandall's estimates of the VER's price effects. Specifically, the authors estimate the prices which would have existed without the restraint by adjusting actual prices by factors which yield the same percent reduction as indicated by the ratio of predicted to actual values in Crandall's study. Once these price changes are made, the equilibrium model generates estimates of its endogenous variables, including quantities of U.S. and Japanese vehicles without the influence of the VER.

Mannering and Winston estimate a steady reduction in quantities of U.S. vehicles domestically sold during the VER period. They find that in 1984, approximately 300,000 fewer U.S. cars were sold

---

[20]See Fred Mannering and Clifford Winston (1985). In this article the term "vehicles" includes cars, pickup trucks, vans and utility vehicles (i.e. Jeeps).

domestically. Despite this reduction in quantities sold, the accompanying price increases were sufficient to give U.S. automobile producers and dealers an estimated $9 billion in profits above what they would have earned without the VER. Although Japanese quantities would have been an estimated 452,000 higher in the absence of the VER, Japanese automobile producers and dealers still gained over $3 billion as a result of the VER.

Thus far, the forecasts generated by Mannering and Winston are for two reasons the most reliable of the studies reviewed. First, the household vehicle choice model used to predict demands was estimated using data for the three years prior to the VER. It is reasonable to assume that consumer behavior which existed just before the imposition of the VER would have prevailed if market intervention had not occurred. Second, the model makes extensive use of information which determines demand and which is exogenous to the market. This feature of the model helps to isolate the VER's effects from other exogenous shocks to the market. There is, however, one drawback to Mannering and Winston's analysis. It relies heavily on the estimates from Crandall's study. The limitations of that study are therefore incorporated into Mannering and Winston's analysis.

Collyns and Dunaway are the only researchers employing EPFM who do not use the results of previously estimated demand and supply equations to determine the VER's effects on prices and quantities of Japanese and U.S. cars. The authors develop a recursive equation system of six behavioral equations and 26 identities. These equations are estimated using annual data for the period 1968 through 1980. Forecasted values of their independent variables are determined for the years 1981 through 1984. The difference between actual and predicted values is assumed to reflect the influence of the VER on those variables.

Collyns and Dunaway explain both the consumer price index (CPI) for new cars and average transaction price for new cars by production costs, fitted values of the inventory-sales ratio, and time trend. The fitted values of the inventory-sales ratio are partly determined by the rate of change in real gross national product and time trend. Real expenditures on new automobiles are explained by real income, real prices (the ratio of the fitted CPI values to the CPI for all items), the interest rate on automobile loans, and the unemployment rate. These four estimated equations enable Collyns and Dunaway to forecast average transaction prices and real expenditures without the influence of the VER. Comparison of the actual to predicted values reveals that, in 1984, the average transaction price increased by $1,650 (or 17%) and the total number of new cars sold domestically decreased by 1.5 million (or 13%).

The two remaining equations included in Collyns and Dunaway's model estimate the relative average transaction price of new domestically produced cars and the share of domestic producers in total new automobile sales.[21] Labor costs and real gasoline prices are assumed to explain the price variable, while fitted values of that variable, real gasoline prices and time trend are assumed to explain the share going to domestic producers. Using these equations together with the model's identities, the authors generate forecasted values of transaction prices and quantities sold of U.S. and Japanese cars. By their estimates, the VER reduced imports of Japanese cars by approximately 1.5 million (or 45%) in 1984, with no significant change in the quantities sold of U.S. cars.[22] In that same year, the existence of the restraint effected an increase in the average transaction price of Japanese cars of approximately $1,700 (or 23%) and an increase of $1,200 (or 12%) in the average transaction price of U.S. cars.

Collyns and Dunaway do not estimate the full impact of the VER on profits. Instead, they evaluate the welfare transfer from consumers to producers. For 1984, they estimate that U.S. producers and dealers captured between $1.2 and $4.9 billion, while Japanese producers and their domestic dealers captured between $1.0 and $5.2 billion.[23]

---

[21]The VER is assumed to have the same effect on prices and expenditures on non-Japanese imported cars as on prices and expenditures on U.S. cars.

[22]They estimate an increase of 6,000 units of new car sales which is only an 0.08% increase over what would have been sold in 1984 without the VER. Estimates for the period 1981 through 1984 indicate that U.S. producers sold 776,000 fewer cars because of conditions created by the VER.

[23]One of the primary contributions of the Collyns and Dunaway study is the isolation of the VER's pure price effects from its quality effects. The pure price effects are those changes in prices which do not reflect changes in product quality or product mix. The quality effects

One drawback of the Collyns and Dunaway study is that only thirteen observations are available for each variable. This severely limits the number of degrees of freedom with which the authors may estimate parameters. A related problem is that the coefficients for the price and expenditure equations are assumed to be constant for a period in which preferences and the structure of the automobile industry significantly change. It is therefore unlikely that the coefficients of the model accurately portray the conditions existing in the domestic automobile market at the time of the VER's imposition. Finally, the market share equation appears to be misspecified. Market share equations formally derived from the cost minimization problem of the consumer generally include real expenditure as an explanatory variable. However, Collyns and Dunaway omit that variable from the share equation for U.S. producers.

2.4 SUMMARY REMARKS

There is agreement between the studies by Crandall/Mannering and Winston and Collyns and Dunaway that prices of Japanese cars increased by about $1,100 in 1984 (see Table 2.1 below). Also, assuming equal quality effects exists, Collyns and Dunaway and Crandall both estimate a $5 billion transfer from domestic consumers to Japanese producers and their dealers. At this point, however, agreement among the studies ends.[24] With regard to the degree by which the VER was binding, estimates range from 12% (Mannering

---

are the remainder of the overall price change. As reported here, the lower bounds are evaluated assuming equal pure price effects for domestic and imported models, while the upper bounds are estimated assuming equal quality effects on those models.

[24]While Willig and Dutz estimate an 18% increase in Japanese prices for 1984, Crandall reports a 40% increase for the same year. It is possible, however, that this difference is partly attributable to increases in retail prices (used in the latter study) in excess of the increases in unit values (used in the former study).

Table 2.1: Estimates of the VER's Effects from Previous Studies

	Willig & Dutz	Crandall	Mannering & Winston	Collyns & Dunaway
Quantity:				
Japanese	-1 mill.	---	-250,000 (-12%)	-1.5 mill. (-45%)
U.S.	+500,000	---	-300,000 (-4%)	+6,000 (+0.08%)
Price:				
Japanese	+18%	+$2,500 (+40%)	+$2,500 (+37%)	+$1,700 (+23%)
U.S.	---	+$1,000 (+10%)	+$1,100 (+12%)	+$1,200 (+12%)
Profits:				
Japanese	---	+$4.6 bill.	+$3.0 bill.	+$1.0 to $5.2 bill.
U.S.	+$0.9 bill.	+$8.0 bill.	+$8.9 bill.	+$1.2 to $4.9 bill.

Source: Values derived from the results reported in the various studies.

Note: Except for the changes in quantities and profits reported by Willig and Dutz for 1985, all values are estimates for 1984. For Crandall, Mannering and Winston and Collyns and Dunaway, only findings for 1984 are given since these authors only reported the VER's impact on profits for that year. Also, these 1984 estimates are chronologically the closest to those reported by Willig and Dutz, who estimated only changes in quantities and U.S. profits for 1985. In addition, there are some differences in the methods used to calculate the VER's impact on profits. Willig and Dutz use the change in quantities multiplied by an estimate of the price-cost margin for a given year. Crandall as well as Collyns and Dunaway use the change in price multiplied by quantities for a given year. Mannering and Winston use the change in revenues minus the change in costs. The last method is the most precise for evaluating the change in profits.

and Winston) to 45 % (Collyns and Dunaway). Although Mannering and Winston find that in the absence of the VER more U.S. cars would have been sold during the early 1980's, Willig and Dutz obtain the opposite result.[25] Notwithstanding differences in the methods of estimation, the estimates of the benefits accruing to U.S. manufacturers and their dealers range from $0.9 billion (Willig and Dutz) to $8.9 billion (Mannering and Winston).

Assessment of the methodologies used in the individual studies reviewed above reveals three common limitations. First, none of the models used in those studies is capable of both estimating the coefficients of a simultaneous system and using the estimated equations to evaluate the policy implications. For example, Gomez-Ibanez et. al. construct a simultaneous system, but not all of their coefficients are determined within their framework. Collyns and Dunaway estimate all of their model's coefficients, but their model is recursively solved. Thus, it is either true that the demand or supply elasticities do not accurately reflect the structure of the domestic industry at the time of the VER's implementation, or that the authors have omitted the feedback effects of the initial supply shock of the VER from their evaluation of the VER's effects.

Second, none of the studies evaluates the VER's effects on profits earned by domestic dealers. Either unit values of Japanese cars are used to isolate the VER's impact on profits of Japanese manufactures, or retail (transaction) prices are used, with no effort made to isolate the change in profits earned by dealers from those earned by manufacturers. Since an accurate estimate of the VER's effect on domestic welfare requires an estimate of the VER-generated profits captured by domestic dealers of Japanese cars, isolating these effects is crucial.

Finally, the assumptions regarding the market behavior of U.S. and Japanese firms in the reviewed studies are either contrary to

---

[25]Comparing the results for 1982 through 1983 for Mannering and Winston and Collyns and Dunaway show that both studies estimate reductions in quantities sold of U.S. cars over the entire period. Mannering and Winston estimate larger reductions over time than Collyns and Dunaway. By 1984, however, Collyns and Dunaway estimate a slightly positive effect on U.S. quantities while Mannering and Winston report a significant negative effect.

previous empirical findings or contradictory of trade theory predictions. For simplicity, most of the studies impose a particular type of behavior on the model without supporting the assumption with empirical evidence. Crandall uses the data to reveal some information about the collective pricing strategy of U.S. manufacturers *vis-à-vis* Japanese producers. However, a presumption about the rivalry between U.S. and Japanese firms still exists in his model.

3.0 Empirical Model

3.1 OVERVIEW

There are three important features to incorporate in a model which would be useful for the current analysis. First, the model should characterize the vertical structure of the automobile industry. That is, the linkages between manufacturers, dealers and consumers must be adequately represented. Second, the model should advance the estimation of structural and behavioral parameters of demand and supply for the domestic car market. Changes in these parameters resulting from changes in consumer preferences and the implementation of the VER should also be estimated. Third, the model should facilitate econometric simulation of market equilibrium under different market conditions. In particular, the model should feature the capacity to predict the prices and quantities which would have prevailed in the domestic car market during the 1980's if the quantity restriction had not been in effect.

The structure of the model used in the present analysis is adapted from successive oligopoly models developed in Pashigian (1965), Greenhut and Ohta (1979) and Bresnahan and Reiss (1985). In such models manufacturers sell their products to consumers through independent dealer networks. Dealers exclusively sell the products of one manufacturer. Each dealer chooses quantities to purchase from the manufacturer such that dealer profits are maximized, given downward sloping consumer demands and wholesale prices. Consumer demands are translated into the demands relevant to the manufacturers through the dealers' optimizing decisions. Each manufacturer, therefore, sets wholesale prices such that manufacturer profits are maximized, given downward sloping dealer demands as well as factor prices. Since the manufacturers are oligopolists, optimal wholesale prices are partially determined by the manufacturers' perceptions about the pricing strategies of their rivals in the market. In the event that manufacturers impose quotas on minimum quantities sold by dealers (i.e., indulge in forcing), consumer demands become directly relevant to the manufacturers' pricing decisions.

The model produces estimates of own- and cross-price elasticities of demand for U.S. and Japanese cars.[26] Marginal costs are also estimated within the model. Changes in consumer preferences for different types of automobiles, induced by gasoline price increases or by changes in attributes of new cars, are reflected in the coefficients of slope dummy variables in the demand equations. The behavior of Japanese and U.S. manufacturers in the domestic market is estimated by conjectural variation parameters. Changes in the slopes of the demand curves and in market behavior are reflected in the coefficients of slope dummy variables. Shifts in demand curves and reaction curves which can be attributed to the presence of the VER are reflected in shift dummy variables. A simulation of the estimated model with the dummy variables related to the VER set to zero yields estimates of equilibrium prices and quantities for the 1980's without the influence of the VER.

As illustrated in Figure 3.1 below, the model is comprised of the following three modules which are solved simultaneously: consumer demands, dealer demands and manufacturer behavioral equations. The equations of each module are developed in Sections 3.2 through 3.4, while the specification of the full model is given in Section 3.5.

---

[26]Only demand and supply relationships relevant to the domestic sale of new Japanese and U.S. cars are analyzed. Prices and quantities of other imported cars are omitted from the model. It is thus assumed that the ability adequately to substitute these cars for Japanese or U.S. cars is negligible. This assumption is supported by the finding that cross elasticities of demand for other imported cars are statistically insignificant in estimated inverse demand curves for Japanese and U.S. cars. The omission of these cars from the analysis, therefore, does not create any significant estimation bias.

Figure 3.1: Schematic of Model

MODULE 1

Consumer Demand Equations
(determination of transaction prices
and of price flexibility elasticities)

MODULE 2

Dealer Demand Equations
(determination of quantities sold
and of demand elasticities)

MODULE 3

Manufacturer Behavioral Equations
(determination of wholesale prices
and of conjectural variation parameters)

Cost and Input Demand Equations
(determination of input demands, of total output
and of marginal costs)

3.2 CONSUMER DEMAND EQUATIONS

One objective of the current study is to determine the extent of noncompetitive behavior between U.S. and Japanese car manufacturers in the domestic market before and after the VER. Oligopoly theory predicts that, when products are heterogeneous, the amount by which prices exceed unit variable costs depends on the degree to which consumers perceive products as substitutes and on the degree to which each firm responds to competitive actions by its rivals. Obtaining estimates of market behavior within the present model thus requires estimates of own and cross slopes (or the corresponding elasticities) of demand curves.

Automobiles have many distinguishing characteristics which collectively determine the degrees to which consumers perceive different car models as substitutes. Ideally, aggregate demand for a given car model should be specified, in part, as a function of the prices of all car models which are close substitutes. However, developing a demand system in which equations are specified for individual car models requires estimation of a vast number of demand slopes (or the corresponding elasticities). It is therefore common practice to simplify the structure of demand systems by assuming broader classifications of substitutes.

Historically, automobile demand models have assumed various levels of aggregation. The earliest studies of automobile demand focused on isolating factors which determine aggregate demand for automobiles. Examples of such models are found in de Wolff (1938), Suits (1958, 1961), Houthakker and Taylor (1966), Hamburger (1967), Hymans (1970), and Juster and Wachtel (1972). All but the first include imports in their aggregate dependent variable; none attempts to explain the demand for imports alone.

In the 1970's, demand models became more disaggregated. During that time, policy makers and automobile industry analysts focused on evaluating the effects that regulation of automobile emissions, of safety and of fuel efficiency would have on the industry and on the economy as a whole. Researchers constructed models that could isolate factors for explaining a given consumer's or household's choice of car as well as the number of cars to own, or for explaining aggregate demand for cars in different market segments.[27] Until the late 1970's, the competitive threat of imported cars was perceived to be

---

[27]Barbara C. Richardson, Lawrence D. Segel, David C. Roberts and Kent B. Joscelyn (1979, 1980, 1982) survey mathematical models developed to study various aspects of motor vehicle transportation. Over 200 models are summarized in the three volumes. Train (1986) reviews automobile demand models which use various approaches of estimating quantities and types of cars purchased domestically.

negligible by both automobile manufacturers and researchers. It was not until 1977 that automobile exports to the U.S. from any single country (for example, Japan) exceeded 10%.[28] In addition, the majority of these imports were small cars and thus did not compete with U.S. makes in their dominant market niche. Thus, the vast majority of these models did not distinguish between domestically produced and imported cars.

By the late 1970's consumer preferences had strongly shifted toward smaller, more fuel efficient cars.[29] Sharp increases in real gasoline prices during the 1970's triggered an increase in the average consumer's preference for fuel efficiency relative to their preferences for capacity, comfort or name brand. At the same time, U.S. manufacturers reduced the average weight of their cars in effort to comply with the Corporate Average Fuel Economy (CAFE) standards set by the federal government and to meet increased demand for more fuel efficient cars. However, average miles-per-gallon (MPG) ratings for domestic cars remained higher than those for imported cars. Hence some consumers replaced their domestic makes with imports.

As foreign cars became closer substitutes for domestically produced cars, policy makers and industry analysts shifted their focus to quantifying the foreseeable effects of import competition on the domestic automobile industry and on the overall economy. In addition, they sought to predict the effects different trade barriers would have on national welfare. Thus, more recent automobile demand models distinguish between domestic and foreign makes.

---

[28]See the 1986 issue of *MVMA Motor Vehicle Facts and Figures*, a publication of the Motor Vehicle Manufacturers Association of the United States, Inc.

[29]Using a technique which estimates the time and duration of changes in the structure of U.S. demand for Japanese cars, Tsurumi and Tsurumi (1983) find that consumer preferences for Japanese cars began to change in late 1976 and that this transition was complete by 1978. David Yoffie (1983) links the shifts in consumer preferences toward Japanese cars to the doubling of oil prices which roughly coincided with the Iranian revolution.

Of the automobile demand models reviewed for this study, only Gomez-Ibanez et. al, Hunker, and Tarr and Morkre report estimates of own- and cross-price demand elasticities for both U.S. and Japanese cars.[30] However, none of these three studies formally estimates all of their demand elasticities within an econometric model. Since estimates of either elasticities or slopes of demand curves for U.S. and Japanese cars are required in the estimation of conjectural variation parameters, the current model must include demand equations for automobiles.

Bresnahan (1989) identifies three methods of estimating demands for heterogeneous products which have been utilized in studies of oligopolistic behavior. In the first method, product choices of individual consumers are modeled given predetermined product segments (discrete choice models as in Schmalensee and Thisse (1986)) or allowing functional distributions on consumer tastes endogenously to determine market segments (spatial models as in Bresnahan (1981, 1987)). Discrete choice models require extensive amounts of data on household purchases, while spatial models impose rigid structures on the form of the demand system. These two factors proved prohibitive of embracing this methodology in the current analysis.

A second method described by Bresnahan requires estimation of partial residual demand curves for the products of a limited number of producers in the industry (Baker and Bresnahan (1985)). The third

---

[30]Neither the 1977 version of Wharton Econometric Forecasting Associates (WEFA) Automobile Demand Model nor the 1983 version of the Data Resources, Inc. (DRI) North American Light Vehicle Model estimate separate demand equations for imported cars. The former sets market shares of U.S. and imported cars exogenously while the latter estimates disaggregate market demands only by size classification. For a comprehensive description of the WEFA model see D. Golomb, M. Luckey, J. Saalberg, B. Richardson and K. Joscelyn (1979). A copy of the DRI model is directly available from DRI. Toder (1978) estimates the elasticity of relative import demand with respect to relative import price. Rousslang and Parker (1984) calculate ratios of cross elasticities to own-price import demand elasticities for twenty manufacturing industries including transportation equipment. Neither of these studies estimate demand elasticities specifically for Japanese imported cars. Tsurumi and Tsurumi (1983) specify aggregate demand for Japanese cars in the U.S. but only estimate the own price elasticity.

method requires estimation of aggregate demand curves for specified product segments where products within each class are assumed to be homogeneous (Gelfand and Spiller (1987)). Either the second or the third method could be used in the present analysis. Since, on average, imported cars other than Japanese makes comprise 5% of the new car market, and since parameter estimates of quantities demanded of other imported cars are either not statistically significant or obtain the wrong sign in estimated inverse demand equations for Japanese and U.S. cars, the second method of estimating demands is superfluous and the third method is therefore chosen. So aggregate demand curves are estimated for Japanese and U.S. cars by market segment.

In trade journals, domestically sold cars are typically placed in one of six categories: sub-compact, compact, sporty, intermediate, standard and luxury. However, in an effort to preserve degrees of freedom, only two classes are presently distinguished--small and large. Sub-compact and compact cars comprise the small car category, while standard, intermediate and luxury cars comprise the large car category. Sporty cars are assigned to a category based on their size. The simplifying assumption is thus that subcompact, compact and small sporty cars are perfect substitutes and that intermediate, standard, luxury and large sporty cars are all perfect substitutes. Since none of the Japanese car models meets the specifications of the large car category over the entire period of the analysis, no distinction is made in the analysis between Japanese small and large cars. Thus, only three types of cars are distinguished in the analysis: (1) Japanese cars, (2) U.S. small cars and (3) U.S. large cars.[31] Cars of the same classification are assumed to be perfect substitutes while those in different classifications are assumed to be imperfect substitutes.

The current discussion of the specification of the consumer demand equations has so far focused on the level to which demands for new cars are aggregated in the current analysis. The remainder of the discussion focuses on the functional form assumed in estimation and on the choice of dependent and independent variables.

Train (1986) places previous aggregate demand systems in one of two categories: those that are consistent with exact aggregation of individual consumer demands and those that approximate systems

---

[31]For further description of the segmentation procedure see Section 4.2 of the Data Chapter.

derived from exact aggregation. Models in the first category impose adding-up, homogeneity and symmetry restrictions on the demand functions. Two examples of these models are Stone's (1954) Linear Expenditure System and Deaton and Muellbauer's (1980a) Almost Ideal Demand System. The benefit of estimating such systems is that the restrictions reduce the number of estimated parameters, thus yielding increased degrees of freedom. However, this benefit is accompanied by a cost: imposing homogeneity and symmetry conditions during estimation of demand functions may be overly restrictive in cases where the budget constraint is not linear or consumer preferences are not consistent. For example, in Deaton and Muellbauer (1980b) the validity of the homogeneity and symmetry restrictions is rejected for a demand system of eight groups of non-durable goods.

Each system also has specific problems. One problem with Stone's framework is that it imposes proportionality on price elasticity and on expenditure elasticity. If this proportionality is not characteristic of consumer demands for automobiles, then using that model imposes unnecessary restrictions on the demand equations. One problem with Deaton and Muellbauer's system of non-linear budget share equations is that they are not readily transformable into the inverse demand equations required for the current model. Other problems with Deaton and Muellbauer's system have already been discussed in Chapter 2 of this thesis.

Apart from the restrictions on coefficients of demand systems, a theoretically derived demand model for durable goods should include an explanatory variable which measures the existing stock of the good purchased for a given period of time.[32] Previous automobile demand models include the stock of existing cars in their demand equations, using a stock-adjustment framework. In addition to relative prices and real income, stock adjustment models of automobile demand regress aggregate purchases of automobiles either on the current stocks of automobiles or on the current stocks of different vintages of

---

[32]Deaton and Muellbauer (1980a) derive the theoretical specification of a simple form of the stock-adjustment model from utility maximization of a representative consumer. See pp. 97-108 and 347-355.

automobiles.[33] The underlying assumption for these stock-adjustment models is that actual physical deterioration of a vehicle occurs at a constant rate.

However, some researchers find this assumption inappropriate for analyzing automobile demand. They reason that the rate of adjustment of vehicle stocks is not constant, but instead depends on the state of the overall economy. In any given year, therefore, vehicle replacement occurs at rates other than those indicated by a constant rate of depreciation. Such detractors from the stock-adjustment model for automobiles suggest, as an alternative, a discretionary replacement model in which the rate of change of economic variables, instead of vehicle stocks, are included.

In order to test which of the two assumptions better characterizes automobile demand, Westin (1975) estimates a stock-adjustment model and a discretionary replacement model for automobiles where the left hand side variable measures aggregate demand at an annual frequency. The explanatory variables common to both models are real disposable income, the relative price of new cars, a measure of existing stocks of different vintages of cars, and a strike dummy. In the first model he also includes measures of the unemployment rate and an index of consumer sentiment, while in the second model he includes the first differences of these two variables. The presence of stock variables reflects the fact that high purchases in one year depresses demand in the subsequent year. The two variables specific to the second model appear as the determinants of postponements and advancements of purchases. Estimation of the two equations reveals that the effects of the stocks of the most recent vintages becomes insignificant when first differences of the unemployment rate (UN) and Consumer Sentiment Index (CSI) are included. However, there is no significant difference in the fit of the two equations. This suggests that first differences of unemployment and consumer sentiment index are reasonable proxies for the measure of existing car stocks in the current model, but that the

---

[33]See Chow (1957) and the WEFA (1977) for examples of the stock-adjustment framework applied in the estimation of automobile demand equations.

discretionary replacement model is not superior to the stock adjustment model.[34]

Thus the consumer demand equations estimated within this model approximate those derived directly for the consumer optimization problem. Since dealers are assumed to set quantities strategically, inverse demands are estimated at the retail level. Therefore, the price of a particular product is a function of the quantities demanded of that product, of the quantities demanded of substitutes and of a measure of total consumer expenditure. Since automobiles are durable goods, the demand equations may also include one or more of the following attitudinal or economic variables: gasoline prices, interest rate, CSI, the first difference of CSI, UN, and the first difference of UN.[35]

In previous studies, linear, semi-log and double-log forms have been used to estimate automobile demand equations. Since there is no *a priori* reason for choosing one over the other, the consumer demand and dealer demand curves (derived in Section 3.3 below) were estimated for each car type using the Box-Cox procedure for determining the best functional form to use during estimation of the full model. The results of these regressions indicate that two of the three consumer demand curves perform slightly better in double-log form than in linear form while two of the three dealer demand curves perform better in linear form than in double-log form. Since neither functional form proved to be predominant in the Box-Cox estimations, and since the double-log form of the demand curves does not facilitate the estimation of the manufacturer behavioral equations with cross equation restrictions imposed from the dealer demand equations, linear demand curves are estimated within the model. Thus retail prices are linearly specified as follows:

---

[34]A test of the validity of these two approaches to estimating automobile demand was not performed for the present study because data on existing stocks of Japanese cars were not available at a quarterly frequency.

[35]Hamburger (1967), Hymans (1970), Juster and Wachtel (1972), Westin (1975), Tishler (1982) and Stein and Beauregard (1984) include one or more of these variables in their studies.

$$P_i = a_i + \sum_j b_{ij}*QD_j + c_i*YD + <d_i,Z> \qquad (1)$$

where i and j indicate Japanese, U.S. small or U.S. large cars, Z is a vector of exogenous demand shift variables and d_i is a vector of coefficients. The notation $<.,.>$ indicates the dot product of the two vectors d_i and Z. The remaining variables are defined as follows.

Real retail prices (P). P_i denotes the price of good i valued in 1982 dollars. This variable measures the average transaction price of each car type.

Quantities (QD). QD_i measures the quantities domestically sold of car type i and is endogenously determined in the dealer demand equations. Assuming that cars are normal goods, that car models of different types are imperfect substitutes and that consumer preferences are consistent, $\partial P_i/\partial QD_i = b_{ii}$ and $\partial P_i/\partial QD_j = b_{ij}$ are expected to be negative. Since the aggregate demand equations are not formally derived from the cost minimization problem of a truly representative consumer, adding-up, homogeneity and Slutsky symmetry restrictions are not imposed.

Real disposable income (YD). This variable is valued in 1982 dollars. Car prices are expected to vary directly with YD since, at higher levels of real income, consumers are able to purchase more of a given product and a different commodity bundle.

The vector Z is decomposed as follows:

Gasoline Price (GAS). According to the Motor Vehicle Manufacturers Association (MVMA), gasoline and oil prices are by far the most significant component of car operating costs. Using data for Israel's car market, Tishler (1982) regressed both segment demand for autos and segment demand for the total quantity of car services on real consumption, real user cost and the real price of gasoline. His coefficients on gasoline for the small car segment are insignificant in both equations--the former slightly positive and the latter slightly negative. This could be the result of opposing effects of gasoline price fluctuations on small car demand. An increase in gasoline prices could shift demand toward small, economy cars. At the same time, the increase in cost of operating a car could cause consumers to postpone their purchases of all types of cars. The sign of the coefficient on GAS in the Japanese and U.S. small car equations could either be positive or negative depending on whether the substitution or income effect is stronger. In Tishler's equations for midsize and large cars the coefficients on gasoline prices are negative and significant. Thus the coefficient on GAS in the U.S. large car equation is expected to be negative. Since the changes in consumer preferences for the type of car to purchase are partly the result of significant increases in real gasoline prices and of the downsizing of U.S. cars during the 1970's, a slope dummy variable is placed on GAS which is equal to 1 for 1979:4 to 1986:4 and zero otherwise. This variable is expected to be positive for U.S. large cars since operating costs associated with the price of gasoline fell after downsizing.

Consumer Sentiment Index (CSI). The CSI is a barometer of the "mood" of consumers, which ostensibly hinges upon their perceptions of business conditions and upon their personal financial situations. The higher the CSI, the more likely it is that consumers will purchase durables, but it is also likely that their purchases will favor large cars. Hymans (1970) finds a "smoothed" version of the CSI to have a positively significant impact on automobile expenditures, probably because expenditures on large cars dominate his dependent variable. Thus no prior expectations are held about the sign of the CSI coefficient for Japanese and U.S. small cars, but the price of U.S. large cars is expected to vary directly with CSI.

Unemployment rate (UN). For similar reasons it is also unclear *a priori* what sign the coefficient on UN will take in the equations for Japanese and U.S. small cars. An increase in the unemployment rate indicates that fewer consumers are likely to enter the new car market, causing downward pressure on automobile prices. However, those that do purchase cars might choose to buy small cars for which initial costs and fuel consumption costs are less than they would be for large cars. Either effect could be predominant. By the same reasoning, the sign of the coefficient on UN in the equation for U.S. large cars is expected to be negative.

Interest rate (IN). The interest on an automobile loan adds to the effective price of a car. Therefore automobile demand is expected to vary indirectly with IN. Hamburger (1967) obtains a negative parameter estimate on interest rates for new automobile purchases, but he uses Moody's rate on long-term corporate bonds and the yield on savings accounts. The interest rate used in the present study is specific to automobiles.

In summary, estimating consumer demand equations within the present econometric model yields estimates of own- and cross-price flexibility coefficients for U.S. and Japanese cars not estimated elsewhere in the literature. These coefficients indicate the change in transaction price which can be expected if there is a change in quantities sold of a given type of car, holding other quantities and demand shift variables constant. Also, since inverse demands are estimated, the model facilitates simulation of equilibrium transactions prices without the influence of the VER.

3.3 DEALER DEMAND EQUATIONS

Automobile dealers are the intermediaries between consumers and producers in the market for new cars. Thus the quantities sold in the market should depend on dealer costs and on the degree of market power held by dealers in the retail market. In the present analysis producers are assumed to hold exclusive relationships with dealers. Thus there are two representative dealers in the model: one which sells Japanese cars and one which sells U.S. small and large cars. These dealers are assumed to be perfectly competitive buyers in the wholesale market and therefore have no power to influence wholesale prices. They also take the inverse demand curves in (1) as given. The unit variable cost of selling a car is assumed to be constant with respect to quantities. This cost includes the car's wholesale price and the variable costs of vendition such as delivery and preparation costs and compensation of sales employees. Within any given quarter of a year, dealers are assumed to sell all of the cars they purchased in that quarter. Inventories are assumed not to exist in light of the difficulty in obtaining data on Japanese dealer purchases. It is assumed that retail prices equilibrate demand quantities and supply quantities for each product in the market.

Pashigian (1965) identifies two limiting cases of manufacturer-dealer relationships. On one extreme, dealers choose quantities which maximize their own profits. On the other, in addition to setting wholesale prices, dealers receive allocations of cars which they must sell and which exceed the optimal quantities they would purchase from the manufacturer at specified wholesale prices.

In the present model, if dealers have market power, it is assumed that they are Cournot-type oligopolists and that they solve the following optimization problem:

$$\text{Max } \Pi^D = \Sigma \; [P_j(QD) - (W_j + S_j)]*QD_j,$$
$$QD_i \qquad j$$

where QD is the vector of quantities demanded, W_j is the wholesale price of car j, S_j denotes additional costs to the dealer of selling car j, superscript D represents domestic dealers of Japanese or US cars, and i and j index the type of cars. A dealer sells either Japanese cars or both U.S. small and large cars. Therefore, for U.S. cars, both i and j index U.S. small cars and U.S. large cars.

The corresponding first-order conditions are:

$$\frac{\partial \Pi^D}{\partial QD_i} = P_i(QD) + \Sigma \frac{\partial P_j}{\partial QD_i} *QD_j = (W_i + S_i) \qquad (2)$$

where $\partial P_j / \partial QD_i$ is supplied by (1) and i, j, and D are as previously defined.

Simultaneously solving the three first order equations in (2) for quantities yields demand curves as functions of wholesale prices, dealer operations costs, own- and cross-price demand slopes and demand shift variables. Dealer demands are thus estimated using the following equations:

$$QD_i = \bar{a}_i + \Sigma \; \bar{b}_{ij}*(W_j + S_j) + \bar{c}_i*YD + <\bar{d}_i, Z> \qquad (3)$$

where i and j are defined as in (1).

In the event that manufacturers set both prices and dealer quotas, dealers will no longer solve the optimizing problem in (2). Instead, dealer profits are driven to zero as manufacturers are able to extract profits from dealers by "forcing" them to buy a certain quantity of cars. In estimation, the demand curves relevant to the manufacturers' optimization decisions still take the form in (3). However, if the forcing model bears a closer relationship to the true representation of the dealer-manufacturer relationship than the unconstrained dealer profit maximization model does, then the demands in (3) are more elastic with respect to wholesale prices in the former model than they are in the latter model.[36] Stated differently, if dealers have power to set quantities in the retail market, then fewer cars are sold than if manufacturers directly encountered consumer demands. This is intuitively clear. For, as manufacturers follow a forcing strategy, they are endeavoring to sell more cars than dealers would be willing to sell at given wholesale prices.

3.4 MANUFACTURER BEHAVIORAL EQUATIONS

In this section, the supply relationships of the model are developed. Because the automobile industry is structurally and behaviorally complex, a few simplifying assumptions are imposed to make the model tractable. It is assumed that Japanese and U.S. automobile manufacturers face the linear demand curves specified in (3) above and operate in perfectly competitive factor markets. Wholesale price is chosen as the only variable that manufacturers strategically set,[37] and weak intertemporal separability of the manufacturers' pricing decisions is assumed. The solution of the manufacturer's optimization problem is static with the dynamic aspect of firm behavior captured by conjectural variation parameters. The objective of each manufacturer is therefore to maximize short-run profits with respect to the wholesale prices of its products, equating marginal costs to perceived marginal revenues.

---

[36]This can be seen by imposing cross equation restrictions on the parameters in (3) from (1). A test of the validity of either model could be performed by imposing the two different cross equation restrictions from consumer demands. However, such a test is outside the purview of this study.

[37]It could alternatively be assumed that in each period manufacturers sequentially choose product attributes (quality) and prices and that a perfect Nash equilibrium exists. Thus a sub-game perfect equilibrium in prices exists given previously determined product qualities. This type of equilibrium is described in Shaked and Sutton (1982).

The assumption that manufacturers choose price as their primary short run strategic variable is supported in the economic literature. Adams (1986) observers the behavior of U.S. automobile makers and states:

> General Motors is clearly the price leader in the industry. It initiates general rounds of price increases; it can, by refusing to follow, prevent either of its two main rivals from leading price alterations; and, finally, its price changes establish de facto price ceilings for Ford and Chrysler.[38]

Caves (1987) concurs stating that there is tacit coordination of prices among U.S. automobile makers. From observing sequences of price announcements in the domestic market during the late 1970's, Kwoka (1984) concludes that Japanese automobile makers competed in prices against each other and against U.S. producers. He asserts that U.S. automobile producers were following a strategy of dynamic limit pricing *vis-à-vis* Japanese manufacturers during that period. Hunker (1983) asserts that foreign producers were the price leaders in the domestic small car market, particularly during the 1970's.

In addition to price, manufacturers strategically position their products in the market by accentuating certain features of their models such as safety, durability, fuel economy, performance and luxury. However, strategies in product quality (features) or product mix are not explicitly characterized here since they are not readily changed in the short run. On average, it takes six or seven years to move a model from its design phase to its production phase.[39] In the interim years,

---

[38]Adams (1986), p. 139.

[39]In the 1960's, the period of time from design to production of a model was approximately three years. However, the CAFE, emissions and safety regulations of the 1970's increased the complexity of model design and tooling costs incurred by manufacturers thereby increasing the length of time it takes to develop a new model. See Adams (1982), p. 158 and Hunker (1983), p. 45.

only minor changes to the model's minor features, such as styling, can be made.

In sum, only strategies in prices are explicitly characterized within the model. Wholesale prices are thus endogenously determined. To mitigate the probability that strategies in product quality incorrectly become attributed to strategies in prices during estimation, slope dummy variables are placed on the parameters of quantities and prices in the model's equations.[40]

Regarding the characterization of firm behavior, at least three different methods have been used in previous studies of competition in a variety of industries: (1) impose a specific behavior on the model; (2) impose a few types of oligopoly solutions on the supply relation and test the validity of each for given time periods; and (3) estimate behavior endogenously.[41]

For the purposes of the current analysis, the first method is overly restrictive. Although the studies cited above indicate that GM was the price leader in the large car market and that foreign producers were the price leaders in the small car market, imposing such behavioral restrictions on the model prevents the discovery of the degree to which noncompetitive behavior existed in the market and the extent to which behavior changed over time. The behavior of firms is theoretically expected to change over time with changes in market conditions such as regulation, entry, mergers and, specifically, VERs. Thus the first method is rejected.

Both the second and third methods take into account the variability of competitive strategies, but the third treats the measure of strategic interaction as a parameter. The third method is adopted in the current analysis because its flexibility facilitates the determination of different types of behavior over time with a single estimation of the model. Accordingly, conjectural variation (CV) parameters are

---

[40]Previous studies have determined that, in response to the VER, Japanese producers followed an optimal strategy of loading the cars destined for the U.S. market with optional equipment (options loading). See Feenstra (1984).

[41]See Bresnahan (1989) for a review of studies representative of each method.

estimated for Japanese and U.S. automobile makers in preference to imposing any common type of firm behavior on all producers.

There is support for empirical estimation of the CV parameters even though its theoretical consistency is criticized in the game theory literature. Friedman (1987) cites three criticisms of Bowley's (1924) conjectural variations framework: (1) it is a dynamic concept in a static model, (2) intertemporal profit maximization by firms is not assumed, and (3) conjectures need not be consistent, the CV parameter being not necessarily equal to the slope of the reaction curve. Geroski, Phlips and Ulph (1986), Bresnahan (1989) and Dixit (1986) all agree that there is a difference between the theoretical and empirical interpretation of CV. Yet they consider the estimated CV parameter to be a true indicator of the type of firm conduct that exists in the market. In particular, Geroski et. al. state:

> Our lack of knowledge of solution concepts can, as a matter of econometric convenience, be parametrized as a lack of knowledge about conjectures. It is then natural to think of such conjectural variations parameters as describing the different equilibrium positions which may have generated the data, but not necessarily as explaining them in a theoretically satisfying manner.[42]

The main advantage of estimating CV parameters is that they assume values which are consistent with known oligopoly solutions. In the current analysis, the CV parameters are expected to reveal the existence of one of the following characterizations of firm behavior: Bertrand, price leadership, tacit collusion or competition.[43] The equivalence of the CV parameter with any one of these oligopoly solutions is illustrated by the following duopoly example. Bertrand behavior is exhibited if each firm assumes price independence, which means that rivals will not respond to a change in its own price. A CV equal to zero is consistent with this behavior. If Firm 1 maintains a

---

[42]Geroski, Phlips and Ulph (1985), p. 10.

[43]Critiques of the assumptions supporting each oligopoly solution are thoroughly presented in Fellner (1960) and in Friedman (1987). Consequently they are not rehearsed here.

Bertrand posture and Firm 2 considers the behavior of Firm 1 in its pricing decision, then price leadership prevails. A CV equal to zero for Firm 1 and a positive number for Firm 2 consistently represent this behavior. In the case of tacit collusion, each firm considers its rival's price response to a change in its own price when setting its optimal price. Positive CV parameters signify some degree of this type of behavior. Competitive behavior is reflected by negative CV parameters.

There are three distinct methods of estimating the CV parameters in the literature. However, none has been used to estimate market behavior of firms in the domestic automobile market.[44] Iwata (1974) isolates the CV parameter from the first order condition of profit maximization for the manufacturers in the Japanese flat glass industry. His calculation of the CV value requires pre-estimation of demand and cost functions. This procedure explicitly assumes that prices are predetermined. Iwata supports this assumption by further assuming that products are homogeneous and that the price elasticity of demand, marginal cost and CV are constant. In Gollop and Roberts (1979) the pattern of CV's across firms in the coffee roasting industry, grouped by size classes, is estimated. Within their model, allowances are made for firms on the periphery of a class to have conjectures more similar to firms on the periphery of a neighboring class than to the average firm in their own class. Since the authors attempt to model the long-run equilibrium behavior of firms, the long-run cost function enters the firms' behavioral equations. The demand for coffee is not specified in their model. Like Iwata, estimates of market demand elasticities are predetermined.

Appelbaum's (1982) framework differs from the two previous models in one notable respect. He estimates market conduct within a simultaneous demand-supply system. His study focuses on the degree

---

[44]Cubbin (1975) compares the reciprocal of the Lerner index to known values of demand elasticity in the U.K. car market, thereby assessing the nature of competition in that industry for the period 1956-1969. Bresnahan (1981, 1987) uses the method of imposing different types of oligopoly solutions on his supply relationships for automobile manufacturers and thus does not estimate CV parameters directly. Crandall (1985) estimates a "conjectural elasticity." However, it is not the formally derived CV parameter found in first order profit maximization conditions.

of competitiveness in the rubber, textile, electrical machinery and tobacco industries. This is accomplished by estimating the annual "conjectural variation elasticity" for each good in a model comprised of input demand, behavioral and market demand equations. The CV elasticity appears in the behavioral equation and is specified as a linear function of predetermined factor prices.

In the present analysis, Appelbaum's approach has been modified. Instead of assuming CV to be a variable equal to a linear function of factor prices, CV is estimated as a parameter using dummy variables to allow for its change over time. In addition, rather than estimate marginal costs within the manufacturer behavioral equations, the cost function is estimated within the model.

Since capital stocks for the U.S. and Japanese automobile industries were not made available for the present analysis, Aizcorbe's method of estimating a long-run partial-cost function is utilized.[45] The long-run partial-cost function is derived by minimizing the sum of labor and materials costs, assuming that capital stocks are set at their long-run cost minimizing levels.[46] Thus the dependent variable of the cost equations measures the factor costs related to labor and materials, while the independent variables are the factor prices of labor, materials and capital as well as total quantities supplied of the different vehicles produced by a given manufacturer.

Following Appelbaum, the cost functions of U.S. and Japanese producers are approximated by the Diewert (Generalized Leontief) cost function,

---

[45]See Aizcorbe (1986) pp. 12-21 for a full description of her methodology.

[46]For the U.S. automobile industry, the assumption that capital stocks are optimally set each period is a quite strong. Gasoline price increases, economic recession and size reductions of large cars which occurred during the late 1970's and early 1980's all contributed to excess capacity for U.S. automobile producers. However, without capital stocks, short-run variable-cost equations would be misspecified.

$$C^F(QS^F_i, R^F) = \Sigma\Sigma\Sigma \; [v^F_{\ell mi} * (R^F_\ell * R^F_m)^{\frac{1}{2}}] * QS^F_i + \Sigma \; v^F_\ell * R^F_\ell \quad (4)$$
$$ {}_{i\ell m} {}_{\ell}$$

where $v^F_{\ell mi}$ and v^F_ℓ are estimable parameters, QS^F_i is the total supply of vehicles of type i, R^F is a vector of factor prices, F indexes Japanese and U.S. producers and both ℓ and m index factor inputs capital, labor and materials. Japanese vehicle output is classified as mini cars, small cars, large cars, trucks and motorcycles.[47] For the U.S., the relevant vehicle types are small cars, large cars or trucks.[48]

There are two advantages to using this functional form to represent manufacturer costs. First, the form theoretically constitutes a second order (local) approximation to any arbitrary cost function. Thus, by Young's theorem, the symmetry restriction applies to its parameters. Also, by Shephard's lemma, differentiation with respect to factor prices yields conditional factor demands which are linear in their parameters. Therefore, the choice of estimation method is not limited by using the factor demand equations to impose restrictions on the marginal cost parameters in the current model. Second, the cost functions are homothetic for all firms and therefore their marginal costs are constant and equal. This allows linear aggregation of quantities supplied by all producers for each vehicle category. For the automobile industry, this characteristic of the cost function is not as restrictive as it might seem. Aizcorbe's (1986) estimation of a quadratic cost function reveals that the marginal cost functions for U.S. and Japanese producers are practically constant with respect to output quantities. In addition, she finds that marginal costs among firms within a given country have similar values. Since marginal costs do not depend on output quantities in the current analysis, the CV parameter is uniquely determined within the behavioral equations below.[49]

---

[47]Japanese output includes exports to the U.S., exports to the rest of the world as well as vehicles purchased in Japan.

[48]U.S. output is distributed between domestic and foreign markets.

[49]Bresnahan (1982) shows that if marginal cost is not constant with respect to quantities, then the CV and the marginal cost parameters may not be uniquely determined in a demand-supply model unless an

Taking output derivatives of (4) yields marginal costs of the form

$$MC^F_i = \frac{\partial C^F(.)}{\partial QS^F_i} = \sum_\ell \sum_m v^F_{\ell m i} * (R^F_\ell * R^F_j)^{\frac{1}{2}} \qquad (5)$$

These marginal cost estimates are introduced into the manufacturer behavioral equations by substitution.

Having discussed the choice of strategic variable, the characterization of market behavior and the form of the cost function, the manufacturers' optimization problem is formally defined as:

$$\underset{W^i}{\text{Max}} \; \Pi^F = \sum_i [W_i - MC^F_i] * QD_i(W)$$

where marginal costs are taken from (5) and substituted herein, W denotes the vector of wholesale prices and i indexes the good or goods sold by firm F. The corresponding first order conditions are:

$$\frac{\partial \Pi^{JP}}{\partial W_1} = QD_1(W) + [W_1 - MC_1]$$

$$* [\frac{\partial QD_1}{\partial W_1} + \frac{\partial QD_1}{\partial W_2} * cv_{21} + \frac{\partial QD_1}{\partial W_3} * cv_{31}] = 0$$

$$\frac{\partial \Pi^{US}}{\partial W_2} = QD_2(W) + [W_2 - MC_2] * [\frac{\partial QD_2}{\partial W_2} + \frac{\partial QD_2}{\partial W_1} * cv_{12}]$$

$$+ [W_3 - MC_3] * [\frac{\partial QD_3}{\partial W_2} + \frac{\partial QD_3}{\partial W_1} * cv_{12}] = 0 \qquad (6)$$

$$\frac{\partial \Pi^{US}}{\partial W_3} = QD_3(W) + [W_2 - MC_2] * [\frac{\partial QD_2}{\partial W_3} + \frac{\partial QD_2}{\partial W_1} * cv_{13}]$$

$$+ [W_3 - MC_3] * [\frac{\partial QD_3}{\partial W_3} + \frac{\partial QD_3}{\partial W_1} * cv_{13}] = 0$$

---

exogenous variable enters interactively with price in the demand equation. However, given that the Leontief cost function assumes constant marginal costs, this problem does not arise.

where $\partial QD_i/\partial W_j$'s are determined in (3) and $cv_{ji}=dW_j/dW_i$ indicates the conjectures entertained by each manufacturer for each market segment. Notice that there are two conjectural variation parameters in the first order condition for Japanese manufacturers but only one is identified. This problem is remedied in the estimation procedure which is detailed in Chapter 5.

The price reaction curves implicitly defined by each equation in (6) are:

$$W_1 = \alpha_{10} + \alpha_{11}*MC_1 + \alpha_{12}*W_2 + \alpha_{13}*W_3 + \alpha_{14}*S$$

$$+ \alpha_{15}*YD + <\beta_1,Z>$$

$$W_2 = \alpha_{20} + \alpha_{21}*MC_2 + \alpha_{22}*W_1 + \alpha_{23}*W_3 + \alpha_{24}*S$$

$$+ \alpha_{25}*YD + <\beta_2,Z> \tag{7}$$

$$W_3 = \alpha_{30} + \alpha_{31}*MC_3 + \alpha_{32}*W_1 + \alpha_{33}*W_2 + \alpha_{34}*S$$

$$+ \alpha_{35}*YD + <\beta_3,Z>$$

Employing the dealer demand equations in (2), the following cross equation parameter restrictions are imposed on (7) by substitution:

$$\alpha_{10} = -\bar{a}_1/\Delta_1 \qquad \alpha_{20} = -\bar{a}_2/\Delta_2 \qquad \alpha_{30} = -\bar{a}_3/\Delta_3$$

$$\alpha_{11} = (\bar{b}_{11}+\bar{b}_{12}*cv_{21} \qquad \alpha_{21} = [\bar{b}_{22}+\bar{b}_{21}*cv_{12} \qquad \alpha_{31} = [\bar{b}_{33}+\bar{b}_{31}*cv_{13}$$
$$+\bar{b}_{13}*cv_{31})/\Delta_1 \qquad +\gamma_2(\bar{b}_{32}+\bar{b}_{31}*cv_{12})]/\Delta_2 \qquad +\gamma_3(\bar{b}_{23}+\bar{b}_{21}*cv_{13})]/\Delta_3$$

$$\alpha_{12} = -\bar{b}_{12}/\Delta_1 \qquad \alpha_{22} = -\bar{b}_{21}/\Delta_2 \qquad \alpha_{32} = -\bar{b}_{31}/\Delta_3$$

$$\alpha_{13} = -\bar{b}_{13}/\Delta_1 \qquad \alpha_{23} = -(\bar{b}_{23}+\bar{b}_{32} \qquad \alpha_{33} = -(\bar{b}_{32}+\bar{b}_{23}$$
$$+\bar{b}_{31}*cv_{12})/\Delta_2 \qquad +\bar{b}_{21}*cv_{13})/\Delta_3$$

$$\alpha_{14} = \frac{-(\bar{b}_{11}+\bar{b}_{12}+\bar{b}_{13})}{\Delta_1} \qquad \alpha_{24} = \frac{-(\bar{b}_{21}+\bar{b}_{22}+\bar{b}_{23})}{\Delta_2} \qquad \alpha_{34} = \frac{-(\bar{b}_{31}+\bar{b}_{32}+\bar{b}_{33})}{\Delta_3}$$

$$\alpha_{15} = -\bar{c}_1/\Delta_1 \qquad \alpha_{25} = -\bar{c}_2/\Delta_2 \qquad \alpha_{35} = -\bar{c}_3/\Delta_3 \tag{8}$$

$$\beta_1 = -\bar{d}_{1i}/\Delta_1 \qquad \beta_2 = -\bar{d}_{2i}/\Delta_2 \qquad \beta_3 = -\bar{d}_{3i}/\Delta_3$$
$$\Delta_1 = 2\bar{b}_{11}+\bar{b}_{12}*cv_{21}+\bar{b}_{13}*cv_{31} \qquad \Delta_2 = 2\bar{b}_{22}+\bar{b}_{21}*cv_{12} \qquad \Delta_3 = 2\bar{b}_{33}+\bar{b}_{31}*cv_{13}$$
$$\gamma_2 = \omega_{lrg}/\omega_{sml} \qquad \gamma_3 = \omega_{sml}/\omega_{lrg}$$

Solving the equations in (7) simultaneously determines the manufacturers' equilibrium wholesale prices. Wholesale prices are therefore determined by marginal costs, the slopes of dealer demand curves and the manufacturers' conjectures.

The cross-equation restrictions from the cost function are also imposed on the marginal cost parameters. They are, respectively:

$$X^F_\ell = \underset{im\ell}{\Sigma\Sigma\Sigma} \; v^F_{\ell mi} * (R^F_m/R^F_\ell)^{\frac{1}{2}} * QS^F_i \qquad (9)$$

where X^F_ℓ denotes the quantities of factor ℓ used in production by firm F and $v^F_{\ell mi} = v^F_{m\ell i}$ by Young's theorem. For the purpose of simulating factor demands in the 1980's without the influence of the VER, the output quantities QS^F_i for the Japanese and U.S. automobile industries are regressed on instrumental variables which are chosen from economic variables of their respective countries. These equations are specified as follows:

$$QS^F_i = g^F_i + <h^F_i, V^F> \qquad (10)$$

where g^F_i is a constant, h^F_i is a vector of parameters for the vector of instruments V^F and i indexes types of vehicles produced. Total quantities produced of any vehicle type does not equal total demand in the U.S. market for that vehicle since some are sold in foreign markets. However, it is assumed that total domestic supply equals total domestic demand in the U.S. market for each quarter of a year.

In summary, the manufacturers face downward sloping dealer demands in each market segment, and with conjectures about their rivals' pricing behavior, set prices strategically to maximize their own profits. These conjectures are not assumed *a priori* to be consistent. In equilibrium, wholesale prices equate marginal costs with their perceived marginal revenues.

3.5 EMPIRICAL SPECIFICATION

The full model consists of equations (1), (3), (4), (7), (9) and (10). However, some of these equations must be modified because of data limitations. Regarding the dealer demand equations, proximate values of the variable cost of selling cars could be calculated only for domestic dealers as a whole. Therefore, S_i does not vary with the type of car sold. Since data on capital stocks were not available for the analysis, the factor demand equations for capital are not estimated.[50] In addition, the data on factor prices and factor demands are only available for the firm as a whole and not specific to the type of vehicle produced. Therefore, all vehicles are converted to a single vehicle type for each firm and their output quantities are aggregated to generate QS^F for either Japanese or U.S. manufacturers.[51]

For the reader's convenience, all of the equations of the model are collectively presented in Table 3.1 below. The relevant changes have been made in dealer demand and manufacturer behavioral equations. The cross equation restrictions in (8) are imposed by substitution; i and j index Japanese, U.S. small and U.S. large cars domestically sold; ℓ and m index the input factors capital, labor and materials, with the equation for the demand for capital stocks omitted; F connotes Japanese or U.S. producers. Seventeen equations are simultaneously solved. The endogenous variables are P_i, QD_i, W_i, X_ℓ, C^F and QS^F, (i.e., 3 transaction prices, 3 quantities demanded, 3 wholesale prices, 4 input demands, 2 cost and 2 quantities supplied equations), while S is determined by an identity (see Section 4.5). The stochastic specification of equations (11) includes time subscripts on the variables and coefficients, and error terms, u_{it}, appended to the equations.

---

[50]Mannering and Winston (1987) use the same sources of cost data, but they use data on total input costs, the total cost of labor and materials, and the price of capital to calculate capital stocks. The risk of deriving capital stocks as a residual is that factor prices excluded from the model could be correlated with factor prices that are included as explanatory variables. Thus biased estimates of marginal cost parameters could result.

[51]More complete explanations of the procedures used to create these variables are given in Chapter 4.

Table 3.1: The Full Model

$$P_i = a_i + \sum_j b_{ij} {*} QD_j + c_i {*} YD + <d_i, Z> \qquad (11a)$$

$$QD_i = \bar{a}_i + \sum_j \bar{b}_{ij} {*} (W_j + S) + \bar{c}_i {*} YD + <\bar{d}_i, Z> \quad (11b)$$

$$W_1 = \alpha_{10} + \alpha_{11} {*} MC_1 + \alpha_{12} {*} W_2 + \alpha_{13} {*} W_3$$
$$+ \alpha_{14} {*} S + \alpha_{15} {*} YD + <\beta_1, Z> \qquad (11c)$$

$$W_2 = \alpha_{20} + \alpha_{21} {*} MC_2 + \alpha_{22} {*} W_1 + \alpha_{23} {*} W_3$$
$$+ \alpha_{24} {*} S + \alpha_{25} {*} YD + <\beta_2, Z> \qquad (11d)$$

$$W_3 = \alpha_{30} + \alpha_{31} {*} MC_3 + \alpha_{32} {*} W_1 + \alpha_{33} {*} W_2$$
$$+ \alpha_{34} {*} S + \alpha_{35} {*} YD + <\beta_3, Z> \qquad (11e)$$

$$C^F(QS^F, R^F) = \sum_\ell \sum_m [v^F_{\ell m} {*} (R^F_\ell {*} R^F_m)^{\frac{1}{2}}] {*} QS^F$$
$$+ \sum_\ell v^F_\ell {*} R^F_\ell \qquad (11f)$$

$$X^F_\ell = \sum_m \sum_\ell v^F_{\ell m} {*} (R^F_m / R^F_\ell)^{\frac{1}{2}} {*} QS^F \qquad (11g)$$

$$QS^F = g^F + <h^F, V^F> \qquad (11h)$$

where $MC^F \equiv \dfrac{\partial C^F(.)}{\partial QS^F} = \sum_\ell \sum_m v^F_{\ell m} {*} (R^F_\ell {*} R^F_m)^{\frac{1}{2}}$ and $v^F_{\ell m} \equiv v^F_{m\ell}$.

4.0 The Data

4.1 OVERVIEW

This Chapter summarizes the sources and availability of the raw data used in this study. It also details the procedures used to transform the data into series required for the analysis. Consumer demand, wholesale and transaction price, demand shift, dealer cost, manufacturer cost, instrumental and dummy variables are sequentially described in Sections 4.2 through 4.8. Summary statistics of the variables which are referred to during the discussion of the results are presented in Table 4.2 at the end of this Chapter.

4.2 CONSUMER DEMAND (QUANTITY) VARIABLES

Quantities of each U.S. and Japanese model which were sold in the domestic market were made available by Data Resources, Inc. (DRI) at monthly frequencies for the period 1970:1 to 1986:12. For the current analysis only two size classes are distinguished: (1) small cars, comprised of sub-compact, compact and small sporty models; and (2) large cars, comprised of intermediate, standard, luxury and luxury sporty models. Segment listings of car models in various issues of *Wards Automotive Yearbook* and those provided by the Bureau of Labor Statistics (BLS) are used when assigning models to either category. A complete list of models by their country-of-origin and size classification is presented in Appendix I.

Given the above definitions, all Japanese models are classified as small cars. Some possible exceptions to this rule are models such as Nissan 300ZX, Nissan Maxima, Toyota Cressida, and Toyota Supra which, by either performance standards, interior capacity or "luxury" appointments, could be classified as large cars.[52] However, since none of these models was sold domestically prior to 1977, a separate category is not created for Japanese large cars.[53]

This study raises the question whether Japanese transplants (cars made in the U.S. by Japanese producers) should be considered Japanese or U.S. cars. Since transplants bear the name of the Japanese producer and there is little or no difference in appearance or sticker price to distinguish a domestically produced from an imported model, it is assumed that consumers perceive comparable models from different sources as perfect substitutes. In addition, the production and pricing decisions for transplants and imports are centrally made at the corporate headquarters in Japan. For these two reasons, transplants are counted with the imported Japanese models. The New United Motor Manufacturing Incorporated (NUMMI) Corolla, produced in the U.S. jointly with General Motors (GM), is included with the Japanese models because it bears the Toyota name.

Certain U.S. small cars are termed "captive imports" because they are produced abroad and sold in the U.S. market under a U.S. nameplate. Whether they should be counted as U.S. or foreign makes in the present analysis is debatable. On the one hand, it is possible that domestic consumers perceive captive imports as having attributes which distinguish them from domestically made small cars--i.e. a higher average level of reliability and higher average fuel economy. If these differences are significant, then captives are imperfect substitutes for

---

[52]Acura Legend and Integra are omitted from the Japanese quantity aggregate because neither BLS nor *Edmund's Foreign Car Prices* reports Acura's prices until 1987.

[53]Although the share of quantities sold of the 300ZX, Maxima, Cressida and Supra in total domestic sales of Japanese cars increased from 0.2% in 1977 to 10.6% in 1986, the largest increases in these shares occurred between 1977 and 1982, and not during most of the VER period. Had it been possible to create a complete series for Japanese large cars, it would have been interesting to note whether the sustained presence of the Japanese in the large car market was facilitated by the VER or by other market conditions such as a fall in gasoline prices.

domestically made small cars and thus should constitute their own category or be aggregated with the makes of their country-of-origin. On the other hand, the decisions on quantities to import for sale in the domestic market and on how they should be priced are made by the U.S. manufacturers which market the cars. However, another dimension of complexity is added to the model if it is augmented to include a separate category for captive imports. Although their production costs are determined abroad, strategic market decisions rests with the U.S. car companies and not with the foreign producers. Thus captives are counted as U.S. small cars. The NUMMI Nova is also counted as a U.S. model since it is sold by GM.

Quarterly segment aggregates were calculated by totaling the monthly quantities corresponding to each quarter and adding these quantities across models in their respective categories. This calculation yields the three car types used in model estimation: Japanese, U.S. small and U.S. large.

4.3 PRICE VARIABLES

The average consumer rarely pays the Manufacturer's Suggested Retail Price (MSRP) or list price for a new car. MSRP is merely the basis price from which consumers and dealers negotiate during the purchase of a car. The price at which the consumer purchases a car (transaction price) is, therefore, partly determined by the level of demand at the time of purchase. During times of dealer overstock, discounts from MSRP are common. During times of supply shortages, such as the shortage of Japanese cars during the VER period, dealers add premiums to MSRP. Thus at the retail level, transaction prices constitute a more accurate representation of market prices than sticker prices.

BLS has calculated monthly average transaction prices for most U.S. and Japanese makes by size classes since May 1979. Prices of all cars purchased during a given month are not included in the price aggregates. Instead, the models which comprise the BLS sample are selected to reflect the composition of the domestic automobile market. The average transaction prices are the sum of the following: (1) base price without options; (2) transportation cost; (3) dealer preparation or handling charge; (4) total taxes excluding sales tax (i.e., gas guzzler tax); (5) total price of options; (6) additional dealer markup (i.e. scarcity premium); and (7) estimated dealer concession or discount--the average discount from offering price or over allowance on a trade-in. Manufacturer and dealer rebate incentives are not included in the transaction prices.

For each month in a given calendar year, BLS reported the transaction prices of two vintages of new cars purchased that year. These vintages are: (1) where the model year coincides with the current calendar year; (2) where, for the earlier months, the model year is that which precedes the current calendar year and where, for the latter months, the model year is that which succeeds the current calendar year. For the years 1979 through 1982, price quotes in category (1) are used for the months January through October and those for category (2) for the remaining months of the year. For October 1983 through 1986, more reliable quotes were found for the next year's models than for the current year's models. Therefore, price quotes in category (2) are used for October through December of those years. This choice is made because fewer quotes for the current year's model are found to be reliable for those months toward the end of the year. It is possible that reliability of the current model year's quotes falls as the next year's models enter the market and are purchased instead of the current year's models.

Not all of the transaction price data could be utilized in this study. BLS has determined that transaction prices based on five or fewer price quotes are unreliable. Their criterion is adopted here. For each make and size class, if all three prices are reported unreliable for a given quarter, then the price for that quarter is designated "not available." If only one or two prices are reliable for a given quarter, then either the single price is used for each month in the quarter, or the average of the two prices is used as a proxy for the missing price. Of course, if all three prices are reliable, no adjustment is made. Those makes, by size classes, which are included in the transaction price aggregates are listed in Appendix II.[54]

---

[54]Since fewer than five price quotes were gathered by BLS for captive imports, transplants or American Motors Corporation (AMC) models, BLS determined these transaction prices to be unreliable and thus they were not used during calculation of average transaction prices.

Weighted averages of these prices for Japanese and U.S. small and large cars are calculated using monthly market shares by make and size class as weights. The monthly aggregates are then converted to their average quarterly values for the period 1979:3 to 1986:4. In two instances, individual transaction prices, which did not span the entire period, are used. In the first, Nissan and Toyota are the only Japanese makes for which prices were reliable for the period beginning in 1979:3. Prices for Honda, Mazda and Subaru only became available in April of 1982. For purposes of comparison, two quarterly series are calculated, one with all five Japanese makes and one where only Nissan and Toyota are represented. At the point where the three makes enter the calculation, the share weights are accordingly adjusted.

Comparing the two series reveals that average prices in the two-make series are lower than the those in the five-make series for the period 1982:2 to 1984:2. With the exception of 1984:4, the reverse is true from 1984:3 to 1986:4. Thus, in an effort to obtain more representative prices for the current analysis, the series calculated from the prices of the five Japanese makes is used. To adjust the series appropriately when prices for Honda, Mazda and Subaru are contributing to the average, a backward linked index of the values of the two-make series is applied to the five-make series for the period 1979:3 to 1982:2.

The second instance in which incomplete series were used in creating average transaction prices occurs with U.S. large cars. Cadillac is the only luxury model with reliable price quotes which span the period 1979:3 to 1986:4. However, reliable data for Buick and Oldsmobile luxury models are available beginning in May, 1985. A procedure similar to that described for Japanese cars above is used to create an average transaction price series for U.S. large cars.

Since the transaction prices are not available for the entire historical period of the present analysis, they are supplemented by list prices from another source. *Edmund's New Car Prices* contains wholesale and retail prices for base U.S. models and for their options. *Edmund's Foreign Car Prices* contains similar information for Japanese cars. Issues of both publications were available from 1973 to the present. Each issue reports manufacturer suggested wholesale and retail prices which were in effect for periods of three to six months. Thus, there are instances in which prices at the individual model level are constant for two quarters.

U.S. and Japanese cars are assumed to be equipped with automatic transmission, air conditioning and AM/FM radio. Accordingly, total wholesale and list price for each model were assumed to be the sum of its base price and the prices of these three options. In some issues, one or more of these options prices were not reported for some models. Unreported options prices related primarily to Japanese models in instances where Edmund's could not collect reliable data for the option, and whenever the option was not available on a particular model. In the former instance, options prices for comparable models of different makes were used as proxies; in the latter, options prices were not added to the base price.

Weighted averages of wholesale and list prices for Japanese, U.S. small and U.S. large cars are calculated at quarterly frequencies for the period 1973:1 to 1986:4; market shares at the model level are used as weights. Although the reported list prices for each model do not always change each quarter, the aggregate list prices do change quarterly as market shares for the models fluctuate. Since the BLS transaction prices are assumed to be more representative of the prices paid by domestic consumers than list prices, the transaction prices are used for those periods where they are available and, otherwise, list prices are used. The transaction price and list price series are therefore spliced. Each spliced series is made by creating a linked index of the list prices for the period 1973:1 to 1979:3 and by applying this index to the 1979:3 value of the transaction price series.

It is possible that some amount of information on price movements is lost by using a linked index on MSRP to extrapolate transaction prices back to 1973:1. Therefore, the degree of correlation between these two prices are determined for each car type for the period 1979:3 to 1986:4. The correlation coefficients are: Japanese cars, 0.90; U.S. small cars, 0.99; U.S. large cars, 0.98. These relatively high correlations indicate that, although transaction prices are more precise in terms of the levels of market prices, list prices are nearly equivalent in terms of variation. This high degree of correlation is also present between the list prices and the transaction prices gathered from BLS. Since the VER period--a period when market prices are likely to vary most from list prices--is subsumed in the period over which the correlation coefficients are determined, it is reasonable to assume that these correlations would be at least as high for the period 1973:1 to 1979:2. Thus the use of MSRP to extrapolate transaction prices back to 1973:1 is valid.

Because the wholesale price and the transaction price series are constructed from different sources, the compatibility of the two series is examined. List prices of base models which correspond to the transaction prices were also provided by BLS. The same aggregation procedure used to create average transaction prices is performed on these list prices. For each car type, average list price is converted to an average wholesale price by multiplying it by the ratio of average wholesale price to average MSRP derived from Edmund's price quotations. The relatively high correlations validate the use of Edmund's wholesale price quotations in this study. The adjusted list prices from BLS could not be used directly since wholesale prices of the options were not disclosed, and the options were not itemized.

In summary, the procedures in this section are used to create average transaction and wholesale prices for Japanese, U.S. small and U.S. large cars, for the period 1973:1 to 1986:4. For the purposes of estimation, these prices are converted to their real values. Transaction prices are deflated by the Implicit Price Deflator for Personal Consumption Expenditures (IPDPC, 1982=1) and wholesale prices of both Japanese and U.S. cars are deflated by the Wholesale Price Index for all commodities (WPI, 1982=1). Both IPDPC and WPI were made available by DRI.

4.4 DEMAND SHIFT VARIABLES

Quarterly data on disposable income and the Consumer Sentiment Index were provided by DRI for the period 1970:1 to 1986:4. DRI also provided monthly data on the interest rate on new car loans for the period 1971:6 to 1986:12. The consumer price index for gasoline (urban population) and the national civilian labor force unemployment rate were made available from BLS at monthly frequencies for the period 1970:1 to 1986:12. Average quarterly values are created for the three monthly series. Data for all of these variables were collected for the years prior to the period of analysis since lagged values are required during model estimation. IPDPC is used to convert values in the disposable income and gasoline price series to their 1982 values. The real consumption deflator is used to convert the interest rate on new car loans to its real values.

4.5 DEALER COST VARIABLE

A source at National Automobile Dealers Association disclosed that the variable costs of a dealership, aside from the wholesale price of cars, fall into three categories: compensation for sales persons, delivery expenses, and policy work (minor adjustments to defective cars on arrival at the dealership).[55] It is reasonable to believe that the largest costs fall into the first category. Therefore, for purposes of this study, dealer variable costs are approximated by quarterly earnings per car sold of non-supervisory workers at new and used car dealerships. These variable costs are determined as follows:

$$S = 12*(R^D*X^D) / (QU + \sum_i QD_i)$$

where S is quarterly average variable cost of selling a car, R^D is average weekly earnings of sales personnel in a given month, X^D is average employment of sales personnel at a dealership in a given month, QU measures domestic sales of used cars and QD_i measures the quantities sold domestically of car type i. Monthly data on employment and average weekly earnings for such workers were obtained from BLS. Since data was not available which differentiated between costs at domestic dealerships of Japanese and U.S. cars, S is used to proxy variable costs at both types of dealerships.

---

[55]The source did not include in this list the interest charges on inventories, nor was such data made available for this study.

4.6 MANUFACTURER COST VARIABLES[56]

For the present model to yield highly accurate estimates of the marginal cost of producing a car, the best available data on the cost components must be utilized. Specifically, the data on factor demands, their prices and outputs should be consistent with actual production functions at the industry level. Published data are available at quarterly frequencies from BLS for U.S. and from Nikkei Telecom Japan News and Retrieval for Japanese automobile industries. However, these data were not sufficient for this study for two reasons. First, it was not clear whether differences in technologies across firms were taken into account when these aggregates were created. And, second, no published data were available which measured the economic costs of capital. Thus a more reliable source of cost data was needed.

Ana Aizcorbe has constructed a data set of factor prices and demand for labor, materials and capital, as well as output quantities by vehicle class, for individual firms in the U.S. and Japanese automobile industries.[57] The U.S. firms included in the data set are General Motors, Ford and Chrysler, while the Japanese firms are Honda, Nissan, Toyota, Daihatsu, Fuji (Subaru), Suzuki, Toyo Kogyo (Mazda) and Isuzu.[58] The firms included in each industry are assumed to have

---

[56]All cost variables described in this section are related to the costs of manufacturing in the primary country of production. Costs related to Japanese and U.S. production in countries other than their home country are not accounted for in this study. Therefore, the costs of producing transplants are not used here. NUMMI production costs are also omitted from this study. The costs of producing captive imports are included in the Japanese averages since Isuzu makes the GM Sprint and Spectrum.

[57]For details on sources of raw data and descriptions of the methods used to construct the data series see Aizcorbe (1986).

[58]Since the production technology employed by AMC was deemed to be significantly different from the technologies employed by the Big Three (GM, Ford and Chrysler), AMC was not included in Aizcorbe's data set. By the same criterion, some Japanese motor vehicle producers

similar technologies. Between industries, technologies are allowed to differ. Thus it is possible to derive the cost variables at the industry level by linear aggregation of the firm-specific data. Weighted averages of the factor prices are calculated for the U.S. and Japanese industries. The weights applied to the factor prices of individual firms are the firm's output shares in their home industry. Total employment, materials used (denominated in pounds), and outputs by vehicle class for each industry are simple aggregates of these variables for all firms in that industry.

Previous studies generally use the interest rate which prevails in the manufacturer's country as a proxy capital costs. But the interest rate is not an accurate measure of the economic cost of capital. A benefit from using Aizcorbe's data is that she includes the factors which are relevant to the firm's costs of investing in capital stock. Such factors are: cost of financing the asset, depreciation, capital gains or losses, and tax savings to the firm derived from holding the asset.[59]

Although Aizcorbe's data are deemed to be more accurate measures of the cost variables than the published BLS or Nikkei data, there are two ways in which her series fall short of the requirements for the present model: (1) her data are only available at annual frequencies; and (2) the series do not cover the entire period of the analysis. In order to utilize these data here, the following procedures are developed to address these problems.

It is assumed that the published series accurately reflect the quarterly fluctuations in these cost variables, while Aizcorbe's annual series contain more accurate values and their long-term trends are more accurate than those of the quarterly series. Thus the average annual values for employment, wage and prices of materials are converted to quarterly values using the following procedure:

1. Identify a quarterly series which at an annual frequency is highly correlated with Aizcorbe's annual series.

---

were omitted from the data set. The only Japanese producer that is omitted from Aizcorbe's data set but included in the demand side of the econometric model is Mitsubishi. Fortunately, all of the producers with the highest shares of the domestic car market are included.

[59]See Aizcorbe (1986), pp. 58-65.

2. Convert the values for the annual series and the quarterly series to their Z values--the individual value minus the mean value for the series, divided by the standard deviation for the series.

3. Match each annual value to the value most nearly equivalent in the quarterly series of the same year.

4. Adjust the values of the quarterly series so that a linked index of the matched values for the quarterly series is the same as a linked index of the annual series. The adjustments are made assuming that each value of the linked index (in absolute terms) maintains its proportion of the change indicated by the two matched values between which it lies. Thus, if a 5% change has to be added to an interval between two matched index numbers, then an intervening index value of 1.02 would be increased by an amount less than another intervening value of 1.04 would be increased.

5. Apply a linked index of the adjusted quarterly series to the first value of the original annual series. This new quarterly series should contain average annual values that are nearly equivalent to those of the annual series and fluctuate from quarter to quarter in a manner similar to that of the quarterly series.

6. The original quarterly series is used to forecast values for the new series out to 1986:4.

This procedure has two advantages. First, by matching values according to their Z statistics, the procedure does not impose a fixed pattern of cyclical behavior on the new series. Second, the long-term growth pattern of the annual series is preserved since the percentage change of the matched values of the quarterly series is constrained to be the same as the percentage change of the corresponding annual values.

With technological advancement, factor productivity is expected to increase over time. In order to distinguish the changes in factor prices caused by changes in technology from changes in demands for the factors, all factor prices in the model should be corrected for productivity increases. Ideally, all factor prices should be adjusted. However, a multi-factor productivity index was only available for the U.S. automobile industry. Since productivity indices were available for U.S. and Japanese automobile workers, only wages were adjusted as indicated in the following procedure:

1.   Indices on labor productivity in the U.S. and Japanese automobile industries were collected for the period 1970:1 to 1986:4. For the U.S., the index used was output per hour for production workers in category Motor Vehicles and Equipment, 1977=100. For the Japanese, the index used was labor productivity index for the category Machinery and Equipment, 1980=100. Each index was converted such that 1982 became the base year.

2.   The natural logarithm of each index was regressed on a constant and time trend. For the U.S., the estimated growth rate factor was 0.7%, while for the Japanese the corresponding factor was 1.9%.

3.   The respective regression coefficients on time trend were then subtracted from unity and multiplied by the appropriate wage rate.

Although quarterly data on production of Japanese motor vehicles are available, they are not directly used here because they include the production of automobile makers not included in Aizcorbe's data. Therefore, to maintain consistency among the cost data in the present analysis, Aizcorbe's annual vehicle output series are converted to quarterly series. Aizcorbe identified eight Japanese vehicle categories which she collapsed into the following five categories: (1) mini cars and light trucks, (2) small cars and small trucks, (3) standard cars, (4) standard trucks and buses, (5) motorcycles.[60] The conversion procedure is as follows:

---

[60]Japanese light and small trucks are not comparable to U.S. light trucks. Therefore Aizcorbe categorizes light and small trucks with cars according to dimension and piston displacement.

1. Quarterly output data from the Nikkei data base are gathered for the original eight categories. Using the vehicle weights supplied by Aizcorbe,[61] the eight quarterly series are collapsed to the five which correspond to Aizcorbe's output classes. Each of the five quarterly output series now has the vehicle weight of the first vehicle named in its category above. Each quarterly series when converted to an annual frequency is highly correlated with Aizcorbe's annual series.

2. Calculate annual output values for the quarterly series and calculate quarterly output shares.

3. For each year, multiply each output share by the difference between Aizcorbe's annual value and the annual value calculated from the quarterly series. This yields quarterly adjustment factors which are then added to their corresponding values in the original quarterly series, thus creating a new quarterly output series.

4. The original quarterly series is used to forecast values for the new series out to 1986:4.

Each new quarterly output series fluctuates like the original quarterly series, but has annual sums equal to Aizcorbe's annual series. Thus the growth rate of the annual series still dictates the long-term growth rate of the new quarterly series.

The annual series for outputs of U.S. firms is not used to derive a quarterly series for the model because Aizcorbe's definitions of small and large cars are not consistent with those used here for demands. Instead, monthly output data from DRI at the model level were available for the period 1970:1 to 1986:12. The output series for U.S. small and large cars is constructed by aggregating monthly values for each quarter and for all small cars, using the segmentation criteria

---

[61]These are averages of weights provided in *Guide to the Motor Industry of Japan, 1982*. The weights for cars are curb weights while those for standard trucks and buses are gross vehicle weights.

described in Section 3.2 above. The cars produced by AMC are omitted from this aggregate since the other cost variables are not available for that make. Aizcorbe's annual data on production of U.S. trucks and buses are calculated from quarterly values reported in various issues of *Wards Automotive Yearbook.* Therefore, those quarterly values are used here. Consistency with the cost data for the U.S. is maintained since the annual values of total car production from the two data sources are similar in magnitude and the series are highly correlated. Table 4.1, below, summarizes the inputs and outputs of the conversion procedures.

The only cost related variables left to be discussed are the capital prices, demands for materials and the dependent variable for the cost equations. Regarding capital prices, no variable was found which was highly correlated with the capital price indices constructed by Aizcorbe. Thus the annual capital price series for the U.S. and Japanese automobile industries were forecasted out to 1986 and assumed to be constant over a given year. The capital price series for the Japanese was forecasted by using the Japanese interest rate on fixed non-residential investment from the Nikkei data base, with ARIMA adjustments for autocorrelative errors. The annual rate of change of inflation and an ARIMA process were used to forecast the U.S. capital price series. The instrument for the U.S. was acquired from DRI.

Following Aizcorbe, the demand for materials is measured in pounds. It is assumed that, for a given vehicle type, the product of average vehicle weight with output quantities yields a measure of the materials demanded to make that type of vehicle. Adding these products together for all vehicle types in each industry yields the total demand for materials in that industry. Thus, the quarterly series for material demand (in pounds) at the industry level are calculated as follows:

$$X^F = \sum_i \omega^F_i * QS^F_i$$

where ω^F_i denotes vehicle weight, QS^F_i denotes output quantities, F denotes Japanese or U.S. cars and i denotes mini cars, small cars, standard cars, trucks/buses or motorcycles for the Japanese, and small cars, large cars or trucks/buses for the U.S.

The vehicle weights for the five Japanese output categories discussed earlier in this section are used here. The curb weights of U.S. small and large cars were collected from issues of *Automotive*

Table 4.1: Summary of Variables Used in Conversion Procedure

Annual Variable	Quarterly Variable	Source	Correlation @ Annual Freq.	Forecast Period
Employment:				
Japan	Production Index for Transportation and Equipment (T&E) (lagged one year)[1]	Nikkei	.96	81:2-86:4
U.S.	Employment in Motor Vehicles and Car Bodies (MV&CB)	BLS	.98	83:1-86:4
Wage:				
Japan	Wage Index for T&E	Nikkei	.99	83:1-86:4
U.S.	Wage in MV&CB	BLS	.99	82:4-86:4
Price of Materials:				
Japan	Wholesale Price Index (lagged one year)[1]	Nikkei	.98	82:4-86:4
U.S.	Index of Input Prices in Motor Vehicle and Car Parts	BLS	.99	82:4-86:4
Japanese Vehicle Outputs:				
Mini Cars/ Light Trucks	Total Mini Car and Light Truck Production	Nikkei	.99	83:1-86:4
Small Cars/ Small Trucks	Total Small Car and Small Truck Production	Nikkei	.99	83:1-86:4
Standard Cars	Total Standard Car Production	Nikkei	.99	83:1-86:4
Trucks/Buses	Total Standard Truck and Bus Production	Nikkei	.98	83:1-86:4
Motorcycles	Total Motorcycle Production	Nikkei	.99	83:1-86:4

Sources: The U.S. employment and wage data are reported in the 1985 and 1987 issues of the U.S. Department of Labor, BLS publication, *Employment Hours and Earnings*. The factor price index was acquired directly from BLS. Nikkei Telecom Japan News & Retrieval is a data base in Japan, supported by Nihon Keizai Shimbun, Inc.

[1] Lagged values of the quarterly series were used since, at an annual frequency, they obtained the highest correlation with Aizcorbe's series when lagged one period.

News Market Data Book. These weights were reported annually; each annual value is assumed to be relevant in each of its quarters. On the basis of the weights of cars collected from *Automotive News* and Aizcorbe's annual data on demands for materials and output quantities, the average weight of U.S. trucks was calculated as a residual.

The data on factor demands and factor prices are only available as aggregates or averages for the firm and not for the type of vehicle produced. Therefore, the factor demand equations are overspecified if individual vehicle types enter as explanatory variables. To remedy this problem, vehicle weights are used to collapse the output varieties into one vehicle type. All outputs are converted to car units, which are comprised of small and large cars. The ratio of the weight of a vehicle other than a car to the weight of a car is used to convert the output quantities of the other vehicles to car units. For Japanese mini cars and motorcycles, this ratio is a fraction. The respective ratios for Japanese and U.S. trucks/buses are greater than one. Total outputs for U.S. and Japanese producers in terms of cars are calculated as follows:

$$QS^F = QS^F_{car} + \sum_i \gamma_i * QS^F_i$$

where γ_i is a ratio of the ith vehicle weight to the weight of cars, F denotes Japanese or U.S. cars and i denotes mini cars, trucks/buses or motorcycles for the Japanese producers and trucks/buses for the U.S. producers. These outputs replace the individual vehicle outputs in the factor demand equations. By construction the marginal costs for U.S. large cars are equal to the product of the marginal cost of cars and the ratio of the average vehicle weight of large cars to that of cars.

Since the costs equations are estimated without the benefit of all the components of capital costs, the dependent variable of those equations only reflect the costs of labor and materials. Thus costs are simply calculated as:

$$C^F = R^F_\ell * X^F_\ell + R^F_m * X^F_m$$

where C denotes cost, R input price, F Japanese or U.S. producers, ℓ labor and m materials.

The yen-dollar exchange rate was collected from DRI at a quarterly frequency for the period 1970:1 to 1986:4. The inverse of this variable, the dollar-yen exchange rate, is used to convert the prices of labor and materials used in production of Japanese cars to their dollar values before they are used in model estimation. Japanese and U.S. factor prices for labor and materials are deflated using the WPI for their respective nations. Since the price of capital in Aizcorbe's data is an index of the real cost of capital, it is already adjusted for inflation. Also, since the current analysis does not focus on the strategies of investing domestically or abroad, and given that the price of capital is an index, the real cost of capital is not deflated by the relative exchange rate.

4.7 INSTRUMENTAL VARIABLES

Real per-capita GNP is used to instrument the Japanese output variable QS^{JP}. This instrument is comprised of the following variables: population (total beginning of month), nominal GNP (seasonally adjusted) and GNP deflator (1980 = 100). These variables were collected from the Nikkei data base at quarterly values for the period 1970:1 to 1986:4.

The following variables were used to instrument the U.S. output variable QS^{US}: real gasoline price, wholesale price index (all commodities, 1982 = 100), real GNP (nominal GNP divided by the GNP implicit price deflator (1982 = 1.00)) and the short-term Treasury Bill rate. All were collected from DRI, and all except the first were available as quarterly data from 1970:1 to 1986:4. The series for real gasoline price was only available from 1971:1 to 1986:4.

4.8 DUMMY VARIABLES

Two types of dummy variables are included in the model: (1) those reflecting periodic changes in the domestic market for automobiles; and (2) those reflecting structural changes in that market. Because demands for automobiles follow seasonal trends, quarterly dummy variables are created--DUM1 through DUM4. For the period 1973:1 through 1986:4, each quarterly dummy variable has a value of one for the quarter it represents and a value of zero otherwise.

There are three significant changes in the domestic automobile market during the period under analysis. First, there was a significant increase in prices of the 1975 model year U.S. cars. Therefore, the dummy variable DUM74 was created to capture this one-time price shift. DUM74 equals one for the period 1974:4 through 1986:4 and zero otherwise.

Second, the gasoline price increases of the early and late 1970's as well as the size reductions of U.S. makes had a significant effect on consumer preferences for the type of car to purchase. A slope dummy variable OPEC is therefore created to reflect these changes. The quarter in which OPEC turns on was determined through experimentation in OLS estimations of the consumer and dealer demand equations. The first quarter for which OPEC equals 1 is determined by selecting alternative quarters of the late 1970's and early 1980's as the first quarter for which OPEC turns on and by then choosing that quarter which marked a long-term change in relationship between gasoline prices and transaction prices or quantities. OPEC is therefore set equal to 1 for 1979:4 to 1986:4 and zero otherwise.

The VER is also expected to have an impact on consumer preferences for the type of car to purchase. These changes may have occurred immediately after the VER was imposed or some years later. To capture these changes in preferences between the pre-VER and VER periods as well as any changes in preferences within the VER period, the VER dummy variables were constructed as follows. Initially, three VER dummy variables were constructed which coincided with the three levels of imports allowed under the VER during the VER period: VER814 equals 1 for 1981:2 to 1984:1, zero otherwise; VER845 equals 1 for 1984:2 to 1985:1, zero otherwise; VER856 equals 1 for 1985:2 to 1986:4, zero otherwise. However, since each VER dummy variable is devised to be interacted with quantities and wholesale prices in the consumer and dealer demand equations, respectively, the degrees of freedom available in estimation would be significantly curtailed. Therefore, the last two VER dummy variables were merged. Given the remaining two VER dummy variables, an experimental procedure similar to that used in creating OPEC was followed to determine which quarters should form the partition of the VER period. The VER dummy variables used in the model are, therefore, VER814 equal to 1 for 1981:2 to 1984:1 and zero otherwise; VER846 equal to 1 for 1984:2 to 1986:4 and zero otherwise.

Table 4.2: Summary Statistics of Variables in the Model

Variable	Variable Name	Units	Period	Mean	Standard Deviation
P1	Transaction	Real $	(73:1-86:4)	7,762	1,106
	Price of		(73;1-81:1)	7,057	560
	Japanese Cars		(81:2-84:1)	8,136	236
			(84:2-86:4)	9,470	803
P2	Transaction	Real $	(73:1-86:4)	7,211	509
	Price of U.S.		(73:1-81:1)	6,906	428
	Small Cars		(81:2-84:1)	7,747	195
			(84:2-86:4)	7,542	163
P3	Transaction	Real $	(73:1-86:4)	10,419	950
	Price of U.S.		(73:1-81:1)	9,718	369
	Large Cars		(81:2-84:1)	11,100	344
			(84:2-86:4)	11,781	425
W1	Wholesale	Real $	(73:1-86:4)	6,381	800
	Price of		(73:1-81:1)	5,836	388
	Japanese Cars		(81:2-84:1)	6,742	381
			(84:2-86:4)	7,624	197
W2	Wholesale	Real $	(73:1-86:4)	6,491	616
	Price of		(73:1-81:1)	6,061	261
	U.S. Small Cars		(81:2-84:1)	6,857	216
			(84:2-86:4)	7,381	416
W3	Wholesale	Real $	(73:1-86:4)	8,537	1,086
	Price of		(73:1-81:1)	7,760	320
	U.S. Large Cars		(81:2-84:1)	9,130	517
			(84:2-86:4)	10,223	567
QD1	Quantities of	Units	(73:1-86:4)	361,295	143,329
	Japanese Cars	Per	(73:1-81:1)	274,828	115,514
	Sold	Quarter	(81:2-84:1)	438,633	33,813
			(84:2-86:4)	536,328	58,995
QD2	Quantities of	Units	(73:1-86:4)	809,673	109,651
	U.S. Small	Per	(73:1-81:1)	812,107	100,554
	Cars Sold	Quarter	(81:2-84:1)	724,803	82,798
			(84:2-86:4)	894,959	97,813
QD3	Quantities of	Units	(73:1-86:4)	1,119,283	285,309
	U.S. Large	Per	(73:1-81:1)	1,219,065	292,904
	Cars Sold	Quarter	(81:2-84:1)	844,943	171,775
			(84:2-86:4)	1,119,217	132,446
YD82	Real Disposable Income	Billions 1982 $	(73:1-86:4)	2,208	229
GAS82	Real Gasoline	Index	(73:1-86:4)	86	16
	Prices	1982 to	(73:1-79:3)	75	7
		84=100	(73:1-86:4)	96	16
CSI	Consumer Sentiment Index	Index 1960:1=1	(73:1-86:4)	0.79	0.12
UN	Unemployment Rate	Percent	(73:1-86:4)	7.25	4.47

Note: Only those variables which are referenced during the presentation of the results are included in this table.

5.0 Results

5.1 OVERVIEW

The model developed in Chapter 3 of this thesis contains simultaneous equations which are nonlinear in their coefficients. For this reason, the model is estimated using the generalized Gauss-Newton method for nonlinear three stage least squares. Estimation of the simultaneous system over the entire period 1973:1 to 1986:4 allows the maximum degrees of freedom and facilitates assessment of the VER's effects on rivalry between Japanese and U.S. producers in the domestic market. Through model simulation, the VER's effects on transaction prices, wholesale prices, quantities, profits of manufacturers and profits of domestic dealers are estimated for the period 1981:2 to 1986:4.

Estimation of the fully specified model reveals that a linear relationship exists among some of the regressors in the model. This multicollinearity problem is manifested through the model's failure to estimate all of its conjectural variation parameters. Therefore, a modified version of the full model, which eliminates the problematical linear relationships, is estimated. The source of the multicollinearity problem and the derivation of the alternative specification are discussed in Section 5.2. The estimation results for the full and alternative models appear in Appendix III.

Although the purpose of this study is to quantify the VER's impact on market behavior and performance, estimation of the model's parameters reveals structural characteristics about the domestic automobile market which previously have not been established through estimation of a simultaneous system. The findings of this study are thus organized into three categories. First, the estimated coefficients on quantities in the consumer demand equations and those on prices in the dealer demand equations are transformed into price flexibility[62] and into demand elasticities, respectively. These elasticities reveal the domestic consumers' perceptions of the substitutability between Japanese, U.S. small and U.S. large cars over the entire period of estimation. By introducing slope dummy variables to the demand equations, changes in consumer preferences over time are captured by the model's coefficients.

Second, estimation of the conjectural variation parameters in the manufacturer behavioral equations reveals the Japanese and U.S. manufacturers' perceptions of market rivalry in the domestic market and the degree to which such perceptions were affected by the VER. In addition, the consistency of these conjectures with actual market behavior is statistically tested. Third, simulated values of transaction prices, wholesale prices and quantities demanded are compared to their actual values to indicate the VER's effects on the market equilibrium in the three disparate market segments. The actual and predicted values of prices and quantities, the model's estimates of marginal cost of production for the different car types and the exogenously determined values of the marginal cost of selling cars at domestic dealerships are all used to determine the VER's effects on profits earned by Japanese and U.S. manufacturers, on profits earned by their respective domestic dealers, on the welfare of domestic consumers and on national welfare. These three categories of results are sequentially discussed in Sections 5.3 through 5.5. All prices, costs and, therefore, profit and welfare estimates are denominated in 1982 dollars.

5.2 ALTERNATIVE MODEL

As previously stated, when the cross-equation restrictions are imposed on the Japanese behavioral equation in the full model, two CV parameters are theoretically derived. The Japanese strategically set the average price of their cars, taking into consideration the responses of U.S. manufacturers in both the small and large car markets. Empirically, however, only one CV parameter is identified. This

---

[62]These elasticities measure the response of transaction prices to changes in quantities demanded.

problem is remedied by choosing to estimate that CV parameter which is most likely to affect the pricing strategy of the Japanese manufacturer. The CV parameter reflecting the response of the price of U.S. large cars to a change in the price of Japanese cars is chosen for the following reasons. Since consumer preferences shifted during the 1970's in favor of fuel efficient cars, Japanese producers were mainly competing for those consumers who previously purchased the larger U.S. cars.[63] Also, as a rule of thumb U.S. manufacturers pegged their small car prices at a fraction below the large car prices. Thus, by observing movements in the large car prices, the Japanese could learn the strategies of U.S. producers in both market segments.

The fully specified model's failure to estimate all of its conjectural variations parameters suggests the existence of collinearity between variables which appear in the manufacturer behavioral equations. Since these equations are derived from the first order conditions of profit maximization, the collinear variables also appear in either the dealer demand or cost equations. In order to determine which of these variables are linearly related, bivariate correlation coefficients are calculated.[64] Although there is a high degree of correlation among the cost-related variables, the cross-equation restrictions from the input demand equations impose nonlinear restrictions on the parameters of those variables, thereby significantly mitigating the collinearity effects. However, of the variables which appear in the dealer demand equations, the correlation coefficients among real wholesale prices, real income and time trend are all above 0.80. Correction of the

---

[63]For the period 1973 to 1986, the share of other imported cars in the domestic market was (approximately) 3 % while the Japanese share of the domestic car market increased from 6 % in 1973 to 22 % in 1986. During the same period, the share of U.S. small cars hovered around 35 % while that of U.S. large cars fell dramatically from 61 % in 1973 to 42 % in 1986. The gains in the domestic market share of Japanese cars is thus mirrored by the losses in market share of U.S. large cars. Although Japanese cars replaced some European before 1973, it is evident that Japanese cars were replacing U.S. large cars thereafter.

[64]It is also possible that there is a multivariate linear relationship in the system of equations. After correcting for bivariate collinearity of the data, the existence of a multivariate relationship was not detected.

multicollinearity problem therefore requires a restructuring of the dealer demand equations.

In the current analysis, the most appropriate method of obtaining a remedy for multicollinearity of the data is to identify relationships among the linearly related variables before re-estimating the model.[65] Of the five variables in the dealer demand equations that are highly correlated, there are only two about which a structural relationship can be specified *a priori*: the wholesale prices of U.S. small and large cars.[66]

Theoretically, profit maximizing U.S. manufacturers should consider the marginal costs of production as well as the responsiveness of consumers and competitors in the relevant market segments when setting their wholesale prices. Although the marginal costs to U.S. manufacturers of producing small cars and large cars are highly correlated,[67] the demand elasticities and the degree of market rivalry in the two markets are significantly different. Therefore, from a theoretical standpoint, wholesale prices of U.S. small and large cars should not be highly correlated. For the period 1973:1 through 1986:4, however, the correlation coefficient of nominal wholesale prices of U.S. small and large cars is 0.99. The correlation coefficient is 0.96 for the corresponding real wholesale prices. It is clear that U.S.

---

[65]See Gujarati (1988) pp. 302-309 for remedial measures for multicollinearity.

[66]Since the model is designed to estimate the pricing strategies of Japanese and U.S. automobile producers, the relationship between wholesale prices of Japanese cars and of U.S. cars cannot be set *a priori*. Also, no prior information is available on the relationship between real income or time trend and the variables with which they are highly correlated.

[67]Since it is assumed that U.S. manufacturers take input prices as given and that input prices do not vary with type of vehicle or quantity produced, and since the relative weights of U.S. small and large cars did not vary much over time, the marginal costs of producing U.S. small and large cars are highly correlated.

manufacturers were not adhering to the theoretically based pricing rules.

Closer examination of the data collected for this study reveals the underlying pricing strategy engaged by U.S. automobile manufacturers. With respect to U.S. cars, the ratio of the average weight of small cars to that of large cars and the ratio of the average nominal wholesale price of small cars to that of large cars over the period 1973 to 1986 were both approximately 0.75. Furthermore, Hunker (1983) characterizes the pricing strategies of U.S. automobile makers as a "constant price per pound per car rule." Thus if the weights of U.S. small and large cars were highly correlated, so would the wholesale prices of these cars. Indeed, for the period 1973 to 1986, the correlation coefficient for vehicle weights of U.S. small cars and large cars is 0.93. It is therefore reasonable to assume that U.S. producers were setting their large car prices based on market and cost conditions, while setting their small car prices at a fraction of their large car prices according to relative vehicle weights.

Apparently, the U.S. producers gave more careful attention to market conditions when setting the prices of their large cars since they were the dominant producers in that market segment and were familiar with demand elasticities in that market. For the small car market, lack of historical information on demand made it difficult for U.S. producers to include demand elasticities for that market in their pricing mechanism. They therefore chose to peg the prices of their small cars to the prices of their large cars.[68]

The dealer demand and manufacturer behavioral equations in the alternative model are therefore predicated on the assumption that the average wholesale price of U.S. small cars is a fixed proportion of the average (profit maximizing) price of U.S. large cars. Although the nominal average wholesale price of U.S. small cars is approximately 75% of the nominal average wholesale price of U.S. large cars, the relationship between the two series changes when both series are

---

[68]It is interesting to note that during the VER period, wholesale prices of U.S. large cars increased at a faster rate than that of wholesale prices of U.S. small cars. This phenomenon possibly reflects the emergence of an independent pricing strategy of U.S. producers for their small cars, given that these producers then had about ten years of information on the structure of the small car market.

deflated to their 1982 values by the U.S. wholesale price index for all commodities. Regressing real wholesale price of U.S. small cars on that of U.S. large cars, allowing for changes in their relationship at the time of price adjustment in 1974 and during the VER period, yields:

$$W_2 = 2003.00 + 0.4802 * W_3 + 0.005255 * (W_3 * VER814)$$
$$(359.10) \quad (0.0466) \quad (0.008496)$$

$$+ 0.005456 * (W_3 * VER846) + 420.00 * DUM74$$
$$(0.01208) \quad (53.32)$$

$$\overline{R}^2 = 0.959 \ D.W. = 0.87 \quad SER = 124.45$$

where numbers in parentheses are standard errors. Removing the insignificant variables from the regression yields

$$W_2 = 1839.00 + 0.5017 * W_3 + 422.00 * DUM74 \qquad (12)$$
$$(131.00) \quad (0.016) \quad (52.20)$$

$$\overline{R}^2 = 0.96 \ \ D.W. = 0.88 \quad SER = 122.56$$

The confidence in using (12) for W_2 in the fully specified model is supported by the high $\overline{R}^2$ and by the standard error of regression statistic. Specifically, the $\overline{R}^2$ indicates that 96% of the variance of W_2 is explained by W_3, given an upward adjustment in the fixed portion of the wholesale price of U.S. small cars. The standard error of regression represents only 2% of the average price of U.S. small cars. With just a moderate degree of serial correlation of the error terms, the fitted series of W_2 tracks the levels and turns in the actual series with a high degree of accuracy. The correlation coefficient between the fitted and actual series is 0.98.

The relationship between real wholesale prices of U.S. small and large cars in (12) is now used to derive the dealer demand and manufacturer behavioral equations for the alternative model. Substituting (12) into the dealer demand equations in (11) yields:

$$QD_i = \hat{a}_i + \hat{b}_{i1}*W_1 + \hat{b}_{i3}*W_3 + \hat{b}_{is}*S$$

$$+ \hat{c}_i*YD + <\hat{d}_i,Z> \qquad (13)$$

where i equals 1 for Japanese cars, 2 for U.S. small cars and 3 for U.S. large cars; $\hat{a}_i = \bar{a}_i + \bar{b}_{i2}*(\alpha_1 + \alpha_2*DUM74)$; $\hat{b}_{i3} = \theta\bar{b}_{i2} + \bar{b}_{i3}$; $\hat{b}_{is} = \bar{b}_{i1} + \bar{b}_{i2} + \bar{b}_{i3}$; $\alpha_1 = 1839$; $\alpha_2 = 422$; $\theta = 0.5017$.

If efficient estimates are obtained for $\hat{a}_i$, $\hat{b}_{i3}$ and $\hat{b}_{is}$, then efficient estimates for $\bar{a}_i$, $\bar{b}_{i2}$ and $\bar{b}_{i3}$ can be calculated as follows:

$$\bar{a}_i = [(1 - \theta)\hat{a}_i - (\alpha_1 + \alpha_2*DUM74)(\hat{b}_{is} - \hat{b}_{i1} - \hat{b}_{i3})]/(1 - \theta)$$
$$\bar{b}_{i2} = (\hat{b}_{is} - \hat{b}_{i1} - \hat{b}_{i3})/(1 - \theta) \tag{14}$$
$$\bar{b}_{i3} = [\hat{b}_{i3} - \theta(\hat{b}_{is} - \hat{b}_{i1})]/(1 - \theta)$$

Thus all of the parameters in the system are determined.

In order to validate the newly specified dealer demand equations, ordinary least square (OLS) estimates of each of these equations were obtained. This procedure reveals that when the coefficient on S (the unit cost to the dealer of selling a car) is unconstrained, then the coefficients on W_1 and W_3 are unreliable. This conclusion is drawn from the results of the following calculation: after estimating each dealer demand equation using OLS, the values of $\hat{b}_{i2}$ and $\hat{b}_{i3}$ were calculated as indicated in (14). These estimates were then converted to elasticities and evaluated on the basis of whether or not they were of reasonable sign and magnitude. The estimates for U.S. cars were either too high and/or of the wrong sign. For example, the own-price elasticity of U.S. large cars was calculated to be 16.3--obviously having an incorrect sign and being too high in value.

In the theoretically derived dealer demand equations, the coefficients on S were constrained to be the same as those corresponding to the wholesale prices to which S was added. If this restriction is applied here, then the dealer demand equations would appear in the model as follows:

$$QD_i = \hat{a}_i + \hat{b}_{i1}*(W_1 + S) + \hat{b}_{i3}*(W_3 + S)$$

$$+ \hat{c}_i*YD + <\hat{d}_i, Z> \tag{15}$$

In effect, the values of $\bar{b}_{i2}$ in the original dealer demand equations are set equal to zero.

The new specification of the dealer demand equations in (15) has two drawbacks. First, the coefficient on S is biased downward by $(1 - \theta)*\bar{b}_{i2}$. This, however, does not present any significant problem in the analysis since it is not expected to affect the values of any other coefficients. Second, since the model will not be able to estimate $\hat{b}_{iS}$, the coefficient on S, all of its parameters will not be identified. In particular, it will not be possible to identify the coefficients on W_2 and W_3. Instead, the coefficient $\hat{b}_{i3}$ on W_3 will be a "composite coefficient" and its related elasticity will be a "composite elasticity." The composite coefficient $\hat{b}_{i3}$ equals $(\theta\bar{b}_{i2} + \bar{b}_{i3})$. Thus, the response in quantity demanded of a particular type of car to the change in the wholesale price of U.S. large cars will include the response to the coincident change in the price of U.S. small cars.

Using the dealer demand equations in (15), the manufacturer behavioral equations derived from the first order conditions of profit maximization are:

$$W_1 = \{MC_1 * [\hat{b}_{11} + \hat{b}_{13} * cv_{31}] - \hat{a}_1 - \hat{b}_{13} * W_3 - (\hat{b}_{11} + \hat{b}_{13}) * S$$

$$- c_1 * YD - <\hat{d}_1, Z>\}/[2\hat{b}_{11} + \hat{b}_{13} * cv_{31}]$$

$$W_2 \equiv \alpha_1 + \theta * W_3$$

$$W_3 = \{\underset{\omega_{avg}}{\underline{MC_{avg}}} * [\omega_{sml}(\hat{b}_{23} + \hat{b}_{21} * cv_{31}) + \omega_{lrg}(\hat{b}_{33} + \hat{b}_{31} * cv_{13}] \quad (16)$$

$$- [\theta\hat{a}_2 + (\alpha_1 + \alpha_2 * DUM74)(\hat{b}_{23} + \hat{b}_{21} * cv_{13}) + \hat{a}_3]$$

$$- (\theta\hat{b}_{21} + \hat{b}_{31}) * W_1 - [\theta(\hat{b}_{21} + \hat{b}_{23}) + (\hat{b}_{31} + \hat{b}_{33})] * S$$

$$- (\theta\hat{c}_2 + \hat{c}_3) * YD - \theta<\hat{d}_2, Z> - <\hat{d}_3, Z>\}$$

$$/[\theta(\hat{b}_{23} + \hat{b}_{21} * cv_{31}) + (2\hat{b}_{33} + \hat{b}_{31} * cv_{13})]$$

where MC_{avg} is marginal cost of producing the average U.S. car; ω_{avg} is the vehicle weight of the average U.S. car; ω_{sml} is the average vehicle weight of U.S. small cars; ω_{lrg} is the average vehicle weight of U.S. large cars. Note that the coefficients α and θ are replaced by their values in (12). For the alternative models, the problem of an unidentified CV parameter in the Japanese manufacturer behavioral equation disappears since the wholesale price of U.S. small cars is omitted from the Japanese dealer demand equation.

Since W_2 is highly correlated with W_1, YD and T, there is reason to expect the coefficients on these variables to be biased when

W_2 is omitted from the dealer demand equations. To estimate the maximum extent of such bias, the coefficients on W_1, YD and T in the full model are compared to those in the alternative model, for all three dealer demand equations. The results of these comparisons are reported in Table 5.1 below.

Table 5.1: Percent Difference Between Estimated Coefficients on Income, Wholesale Price of Japanese Cars and Time Trend

	YD	W_1	T
QD1	- 3	- 4	na
QD2	7	17[a]	na
QD3	-83[a]	674[a]	134[a]

a. This represents a significant percentage change resulting from the omission of W_2 from the dealer demand equations. See Appendix II for the actual values of the coefficients used to calculate these elasticities.

Taking ten percent as the threshold of significant difference, Table 5.1 shows that omitting W_2 from the dealer demand equations has a significant effect on four of the seven coefficients in question. Of those four, the coefficients on W_1 in QD_2 (the dealer demand equation for U.S. small cars) and on T in QD_3 (the dealer demand equation for U.S. large cars) remain statistically insignificant. When W_2 is omitted from the dealer demand equation for U.S. large cars, the coefficient on W_1 becomes significant and the coefficient on YD becomes insignificant. Although there is no need for concern regarding changes in the first two coefficients, the significant changes in the last two warrant further investigation.

Calculation of price elasticity of demand with respect to W_1 and of the income elasticity for the dealer demand equation for U.S. large cars are given in Table 5.2 below. It is evident from these elasticities that the alternative model produces a more realistic estimate of the

**Table 5.2: Price and Income Elasticities
of Demand for U.S. Large Cars**

	Full Model	Alternative Model
$\dfrac{\partial QD_3}{\partial W_1} \dfrac{W_1}{QD_3}$	0.14	1.07
$\dfrac{\partial QD_3}{\partial YD} \dfrac{YD}{QD_3}$	1.40	0.30

coefficient on W_1 in the dealer demand equation for U.S. large cars than the full model does and that the full model is more accurate at estimating the coefficient on YD in that equation. Since the accuracy with which the model estimates the price coefficients is more important to the current analysis than the efficiency with which it estimates income coefficients, the results generated by the alternative model are deemed acceptable and are reported in Section 5.3 below.

5.3 PRICE FLEXIBILITY AND DEMAND ELASTICITIES

Since price is regressed on quantities in the inverse consumer demand equations, calculation of the traditional demand elasticities at the retail level is prohibited.[69] Thus, for purposes of discussion, the coefficients on quantities in the consumer demand equations are converted into price flexibility elasticities. In order to compare the current results to those of any previous study, the coefficients on wholesale prices in the dealer demand equations are converted into

---

[69]Applying Cramer's rule to the consumer demand equations does not produce accurate coefficients for computing the typical demand elasticities since, unlike the case for direct demand curves, different variables are held constant when inverse demand curves are being estimated.

traditional demand elasticities. But, before presenting these results, the methods used to detect changes over time in the slopes of the demand curves are described.

Theoretically, the demand curves for automobiles are in part determined by product quality and by consumer expectations regarding supplies. Thus, through its effects on product quality and on consumer expectations, the VER could have caused the demand curves for the different classes of car models to change slope and to shift. Unfortunately, it is not practical to include variables representing product quality and consumer expectations in the specification of the demand equations. Thus, in order to capture the quality and expectations effects of the VER, dummy variables representing the VER period are devised to interact with quantities in the consumer demand equations and with wholesale prices in the dealer demand equations.[70] In addition, VER dummy variables are included as shift dummy variables in both sets of demand equations. Thus the position of each demand curve is allowed to change between the pre-VER and VER periods, and, in order to allow for lags in the quality effect or for unfulfilled expectations, the position is also allowed to change during the VER period. Specifically, two dummy variables are established to represent the presence of the VER: VER814 equals 1 for 1981:2 to 1984:1 and 0 otherwise; VER846 equals 1 for 1984:2 to 1986:4 and 0 otherwise. In all, three periods are distinguished during estimation: pre-VER, early VER and late VER. It is therefore possible for a given quantity or price to have three different coefficients.

All elasticities reported below are calculated using the average price and quantity corresponding to the slope coefficient used. For example, if the own-price demand elasticity for U.S. large cars is calculated for 1973:1 to 1981:1, then the slope coefficient b_{33} is multiplied by the ratio of the average wholesale price and average

---

[70]It is possible that decisions by the manufacturers, independent of the VER, are responsible for some percentage of the quality change. For instance, some of the product quality increments in Japanese cars or the introduction of their upscale models could have been planned before the VER took effect. Since the current framework does not allow the VER effects on product quality to be distinguished from already planned model changes, the model could overestimate the VER's impact on demand elasticities.

quantities sold of U.S. large cars for the same period. As a test to see whether the use of average prices and quantities exaggerated the difference between periods of a given elasticity, the median values of prices and quantities were also used to calculate the elasticities. Both methods yielded the same values for the price flexibility elasticities. For the demand elasticities, in the cases where significant differences in values occur between the two methods, the qualitative results remain unchanged.

Since the domestic consumers of Japanese cars are rationed in the market (i.e. the VER is binding), estimating the dealer demand equation representing Japanese cars over the entire period requires special consideration. One possible approach is to impose the restraint on quantities imported of Japanese cars directly on the model. However, this method becomes problematical since some Japanese cars were made or assembled and sold domestically (though too few in quantity to make the VER non-binding). So instead, dummy variables for each quarter of the period 1981:2 to 1986:4 are included in the Japanese dealer demand equation. Therefore, the estimated coefficients of wholesale prices in that equation are those pertaining to the period before the VER. This does not present a problem when the estimates are used for simulating the activities of the 1980's without the effects of the VER. However, since these coefficients partly determine the Japanese CV parameter, the estimate of that parameter could be biased.

The majority of price flexibility elasticities estimated by the model have a negative sign as expected, indicating that the three types of cars distinguished in this study are substitutes (see Table 5.3 below). The price flexibility elasticities that have a positive sign are either calculated from coefficients that are not significantly different from zero or reflect short-run effects of quality enhancement or pent-up demand caused by the VER.

Thus, for the pre-VER period, the price flexibility elasticities indicate that Japanese transaction prices were more responsive to a change in quantities sold of Japanese cars than were U.S. large car prices to a change in quantities sold of U.S. large cars. In the average quarter of the pre-VER period, a 10% (27-thousand-car) increase in quantities sold of Japanese cars during the pre-VER period would require a 1.3% ($90) reduction in the transaction price of Japanese cars, while the same percentage increase in quantities sold of U.S.

Table 5.3: Price Flexibility Elasticities

		1973:1 - 1981:1	
	QD1	**QD2**	**QD3**
P1	-0.13	-0.02*	-0.08
P2	-0.04	0.02*	-0.10
P3	-0.007*	-0.07	-0.07
		1981:2 - 1984:1	
	QD1	**QD2**	**QD3**
P1	-0.05	-0.02*	-0.19
P2	-0.06	0.02*	-0.14
P3	-0.01*	-0.05	0.03
		1984:2 - 1986:4	
	QD1	**QD2**	**QD3**
P1	0.16	-0.02*	-0.05
P2	-0.08	0.03*	-0.08
P3	0.09	-0.06	-0.05

An asterisk (*) indicates statistically insignificant elasticities.

large cars (122 thousand cars) would only require a 0.7% ($70)[71] reduction in the transaction price of U.S. large cars.[72] These findings are consistent with the fact that, prior to the VER, Japanese manufacturers were endeavoring to penetrate the U.S. market.

Since the majority of their customers would be first time buyers of Japanese cars, domestic dealers of Japanese cars were likely to negotiate with customers on price in order to increase their market share. However, U.S. manufacturers were the dominant producer in the large cars market. Since repurchase rates on U.S. cars were over 70% during that period,[73] an owner of a U.S. car was likely to replace that car with another U.S. car (most likely of the same make). Thus, U.S. manufacturers would be less likely to negotiate with customers on price.

There are, however, asymmetries among the cross price flexibility elasticities. While transaction prices of U.S. large cars are not responsive to quantities sold of Japanese cars, transaction prices of Japanese cars are responsive to quantities sold of U.S. large cars. In addition, transaction prices of U.S. small cars are responsive to quantities sold of Japanese cars, but transaction prices of Japanese cars are not responsive to quantities sold of U.S. small cars.

These asymmetries could be explained as follows. On the one hand, U.S. producers were slow to respond to the Japanese threat to their market share. When the U.S. producers responded, they developed their small cars to compete with Japanese cars. Dealers of U.S. cars would therefore be more willing to negotiate with consumers on the prices of their small cars than on the prices of their large cars in response to an increase in quantities sold of Japanese cars. On the other hand, Japanese entry into the U.S. car market coincided with the

---

[71]The own price response for U.S. small cars is positive but not significantly different from zero.

[72]Unless otherwise stated, all percentages, prices, quantities and intertemporal comparisons referenced in the following discussion on price flexibility and demand elasticities pertain to average quarters of a given period.

[73]The repurchase rates are based on Customer Satisfaction Indices comprised by J.D. Power and Associates, 1981 to 1986.

first oil crisis of the 1970's. Since, in the consumer's view, qualitatively and functionally competitive U.S. small cars were not yet being sold, marginal consumers of U.S. large cars who wanted to economize on fuel consumption found Japanese cars to be the suitable alternative. Thus, a 10% increase in quantities of U.S. large cars caused a 0.8% ($60) decrease in transaction prices of Japanese cars, while a 10% increase in quantities of Japanese cars caused a 0.07% ($7)[74] decrease in the transaction prices of U.S. large cars. Transaction prices of Japanese cars would fall by only 0.2% ($15) given a 10% increase in quantities sold of U.S. small cars, while a similar increase in quantities sold of Japanese cars would cause a 0.4% ($30) decrease in the transaction prices of U.S. small cars. Since transaction prices are jointly determined by consumers and producers during the purchasing of a car, the asymmetry becomes established by the perceptions of both consumers and producers who differ on which types of cars are closer substitutes.

As indicated by the price flexibility elasticities, there was a significant change in the position of some consumer demand curves during the VER regime. During the early VER period (1981:2 to 1984:1), the most significant changes in price flexibility elasticities indicate a decrease in the responsiveness of Japanese transaction prices to its own quantity and a change in sign from negative to positive for the responsiveness of U.S. large cars to its own quantity. In particular, a 0.5% ($40) decrease in the transaction price of Japanese cars would accompany a 10% (44-thousand-car) increase in quantities sold of those cars, while a 0.3% ($30) increase in the transaction price of U.S. large cars would accompany a 10% (85-thousand-car) increase in quantities of U.S. large cars sold. These changes can be interpreted as follows.[75]

---

[74]Not significantly different from zero.

[75]The mean quantity of Japanese cars sold during a quarter increased by 60% from the pre-VER period to the early VER period, and by 22% from the early VER period to the late VER period. Since the price flexibility elasticities represent the ratio of the percentage change in price to percentage change in quantity, if the demand curves maintained the same slope from period to period, the increase in quantities would be consistent with an increase in elasticity. However, the change in position of the consumer demand curve for Japanese cars

When the VER was imposed, demand exceeded supply for Japanese cars in the domestic market. Thus, domestic dealers of Japanese cars could exact higher prices from their consumers for the available cars. Quality upgrading also contributed to higher transaction prices for cars and thus to a lower responsiveness of Japanese transaction prices to changes in quantities sold. Some of the potential Japanese car customers (either previous owners of Japanese cars, owners of U.S. cars or potential first-time car buyers), were unable to purchase the car of their choice. These customers had two choices. One, they could wait until more models were made available either because a scheduled shipment had landed in the U.S. or because the VER was rescinded.[76] Or, two, consumers could purchase a U.S. make. The U.S. make was likely to be in the large car class since U.S. manufacturers had reduced the average size of their large cars. Their small cars were either of unreliable quality or imported from Japan and thus in limited supply since captive imports were included in the VER. Thus, during the early stage of the VER, U.S. producers could command a higher price for a given quantity of their large cars because of pent-up demand for automobiles.

During the late VER period (1984:2 to 1986:4), the price flexibility elasticity for U.S. large cars with respect to own quantity return to (approximately) its pre-VER level, thus a 10% (112-thousand-car) increase in own quantity caused a 0.5% ($60) decrease in its price. But the price flexibility elasticity for Japanese cars with respect to own

---

together with the change in supply leads to the opposite effect on their price flexibility elasticities. Although the mean quantity sold during a quarter of U.S. large cars fell by 70% from the pre-VER period to the early VER period, changes in the position of the demand curve together with supply shifts account for the marked change in price flexibility elasticity. During the late VER period, quantities sold of U.S. large cars rebounded by 33% and the corresponding elasticity returned to approximately its pre-VER level. Note that the effects of the recession of the early 1980's are captured by real income, the consumer sentiment index and the unemployment rate which are included in the demand equations.

[76]Initially, the VER was only supposed to last for two, at most three years.

quantity turned positive: a 10% (54-thousand-car) increase in own quantity was consistent with a 1.6% ($150) increase in transaction price. These elasticities indicate that U.S. manufacturers could have only benefitted from a one-time shift of consumers from Japanese cars to U.S. large cars (or from the prevention of further abandonment by their customers) during the early stage of the VER. Even if the marginal Japanese car customers switched to U.S. large cars, the inframarginal Japanese car customers postponed their car purchases until Japanese cars were available.[77] Furthermore, increased quality in the form of more standard equipment and larger capacity as well as pent-up demand increased the average transaction price during the VER by so much that, although more Japanese cars were imported during the late VER period, an increase in quantities sold of Japanese cars was still consistent with an increase in transaction prices for those cars.

In summary, by creating a shortage in supply of Japanese cars and by inducing a change in product quality, the VER triggered a change in the positions of consumer demand curves for Japanese and U.S. large cars. During the early period of the VER, the demand curve for U.S. large cars became positive. But this was only a short lived phenomenon as that demand curve shifted outward owing to the initial reduction in quantities of Japanese cars.[78] In the long run, the demand curve for U.S. producers resumed its negative slope. Since Japanese cars were rationed during the entire VER period, the demand curves for Japanese cars did not settle at a new level during the period under analysis. Thus the price flexibility elasticities continue to indicate a repositioning of the demand curve for Japanese cars.

While the price flexibility elasticities reflect price responses, holding quantities constant, the demand elasticities reported in Table 5.4 below reflect the responsiveness of quantities demanded to changes

---

[77]The J.D. Power and Associates' Customer Satisfaction Indices show a domestic repurchase rate for Japanese cars of approximately 85% for 1983 through 1986. For the years prior to 1983, J.D. Power did not distinguish Japanese cars other imported cars in comprising their Customer Satisfaction Index.

[78]Note that these are partial effects. As will be discussed later, the economic recession of the early 1980's had the opposite effect of shifting in the demand curve for U.S. large cars.

Table 5.4: Dealer Demand Elasticities

	1973:1 - 1981:1	
	W1	**W3**
QD1	-3.65	2.20
QD2	-0.25*	-0.16*
QD3	0.90	-1.69
	1981:2 - 1984:1	
	W1	**W3**
QD1	-2.64	1.62
QD2	-0.33*	-0.44*
QD3	1.49	-2.87
	1984:2 - 1986:4	
	W1	**W3**
QD1	-2.45	1.49
QD2	-0.30*	-0.25*
QD3	1.27	-2.43

An asterisk (*) indicates statistically insignificant elasticities.

Note: All of the elasticities in the column for W_3 are composite elasticities and thus include a partial effect of the change in W_2 which accompanies a change in W_3. Those elasticities therefore represent the total effect on quantities of a change in W_3 by the U.S. producers but do not include the effect W_3 has on W_1.

in wholesale price holding other wholesale prices and demand shift variables constant. With the exception of the coefficient on quantities of U.S. large cars in the dealer demand curve for U.S. small cars, none of the coefficients on quantities in the dealer demand equations is affected by the VER. Since the dealer demand equation for Japanese cars includes dummy variables for all quarters of the VER period, it is not possible to detect changes in its slope resulting from quality enhancement caused by the VER. However, it might seem peculiar that the slope of the dealer demand curve for U.S. large cars was unaffected by the VER given that the consumer demand equations for these cars were affected. One possible explanation for this occurrence is that, while transaction prices include the costs of all options purchased, the wholesale price series for U.S. cars includes the costs of the same options for the pre-VER and VER periods. Thus, if U.S. producers enhanced product quality by making more options standard on their cars, the wholesale price series would not reflect this action. However, the wholesale price series of U.S. cars would reflect any increase in price owing to increases in fit and finish, in reliability or in capacity. To the extent that the latter means of increasing product quality was adopted by the U.S. producers, the estimated dealer demand equation for U.S. large cars indicates that such changes did not have a significant effect on the relationship between quantities sold of U.S. large cars and their wholesale price. Thus by 1986, any increases in reliability of U.S. cars had not yet been perceived by the market.

Although the slopes on the dealer demand equations for Japanese and U.S. large cars do not vary with the VER, the corresponding demand elasticities do vary over time as the ratio of prices to quantities changes. Specifically, the own-price elasticity of demand for Japanese cars and that for U.S. large cars indicate that quantities sold of the former were more responsive than quantities sold of the latter to changes in their respective wholesale prices during the pre-VER period. A 1% ($60) increase in the wholesale price of Japanese cars would cause a 3.7% (10-thousand-car) decrease in quantities sold of Japanese cars, while a 1% ($80) increase in the wholesale price of U.S. large cars would cause a 1.7% (21-thousand-car) decrease in quantities sold of U.S. large cars. This behavior is again consistent with the scenario that depicts the U.S. as the incumbent producers while the Japanese were in the process of penetrating the domestic market.

During the early VER period, the responsiveness of quantities of U.S. large cars to own price slightly exceeded that for the Japanese. A

1% increase in own price ($90 for U.S. large cars and $70 for Japanese cars) caused a 2.8% (24-thousand-car) decrease in quantities of U.S. large cars sold and a 2.6% (11-thousand-car) decrease in quantities sold of Japanese cars. But, by the late VER period, the responses of quantities sold of U.S. large cars and Japanese cars to a 1% increase in the respective wholesale prices ($100 and $80, respectively) were approximately the same--a 2.5% decrease (28 thousand and 13 thousand cars, respectively).

Since the model is not able to detect changes in the slope of the dealer demand equations for Japanese cars with respect to wholesale prices, the full VER effects are not captured by these elasticities. What is reflected here is that, although quantity restraints were binding with respect to what the Japanese could have sold,[79] quantities sold during the VER increased from their pre-VER levels. In the average quarter during the early VER period, 60% more Japanese cars were sold than in the average quarter of the pre-VER period and 23% more were sold during the average quarter of the late VER period than in the early VER period. This increase in quantities would place Japanese dealers on the more inelastic portion of their demand curves. It is true that wholesale prices also rose from period to period (15.5% from pre-VER to early VER and 13% from early VER to late VER) but, without detectable changes in the slopes of the demand curves, the quantity increases dominated the price increases during calculation of the own-price elasticities for Japanese cars, resulting in their decrease over time.[80]

Similarly, for U.S. large cars, the increase in responsiveness of quantities to own price is attributed to the fact that quantities sold decreased by 70% while wholesale prices increased by 18% between

---

[79]Evidence of the degree to which the VER was binding is reported in Section 5.5.

[80]The lower elasticities during the VER period are, however, consistent with the existence of rationed quantities of Japanese cars, since changes in their wholesale prices would no longer have as great an effect on the quantities purchased. A reduction in the wholesale price of Japanese cars could not increase quantities sold above the quota. Similarly, an increase in their prices would not deter many customers from purchasing Japanese cars since excess demand existed.

the pre-VER and the early VER periods. Between the early and late VER periods, quantities increased by 30%, while wholesale prices increased by 12%. Thus, given that the slopes of the dealer demand curve did not change during the VER period, the fall in quantities and rise in wholesale prices between the pre-VER period and entire VER period placed dealers of U.S. large cars on the more elastic portion of their demand curves. The increase in the price elasticity for U.S. large cars at the wholesale level could in part be a result of the VER if U.S. manufacturers increased their prices, given that quantities of Japanese cars were constrained.

The cross price elasticities for the dealer demand curves confirm the findings for the consumer demand equations that Japanese and U.S. large cars are substitutes. These elasticities also indicate that, during the pre-VER period, Japanese quantities were more responsive to changes in wholesale prices of U.S. large cars than were U.S. large car quantities to changes in the wholesale prices of Japanese cars. For example, a 1% increase in the wholesale price of U.S. large cars caused a 2.5% (7-thousand-car) increase in quantities of Japanese cars, while a similar percentage increase in the price of Japanese cars caused a 0.9% (11-thousand-car) increase in quantities of U.S. large cars.

With the VER, the responsiveness of Japanese and U.S. quantities to changes in wholesale prices of the competing product became approximately equal. In the early VER period, cross price elasticities for Japanese and U.S. large cars were 1.6 and 1.5, respectively, and, in the late VER period, they were 1.5 and 1.3, respectively. Japanese quantities became less responsive to changes in U.S. wholesale prices, while U.S. large cars quantities became more responsive to changes in Japanese wholesale prices. Thus as the Japanese expanded market share in the U.S., dealer demands became more symmetric.

Apart from the VER, consumer preferences for cars were affected by other exogenous factors during the period of current analysis. The most noted occurrences were the two gasoline price shocks of the 1970's which raised the cost to the consumer of operating a vehicle and caused U.S. automobile manufacturers to downsize the cars in their product lines. It should be recalled that the slope dummy variable OPEC was included in Section 4.8 of Chapter 4 to account for these effects within the model. Thus two periods are distinguished for gasoline price levels.

There are two opposing effects that are expected to accompany a gasoline price increase. One, since gasoline is a variable cost of operating a car, an increase in gasoline prices is expected to have a negative effect on quantities purchased. Two, an increase in the price of gasoline could have a positive effect on quantities purchased of smaller cars, since they are more fuel efficient and therefore cheaper to operate than larger cars. Therefore, the estimated coefficient for GAS is expected to be negative for U.S. large cars, but there is no prior expectation on that coefficient for Japanese or for small U.S. cars since both the negative and positive effects of a change in gasoline prices are expected to be present. The estimated coefficient of OPEC is expected to be positive for U.S. large cars as size reductions in the late 1970's, which were necessary for U.S. manufacturers to comply with the CAFE standards, made those cars cheaper to operate. For Japanese cars and U.S. small cars, there is no prior expectation on the OPEC parameter.

Although GAS and OPEC enter both the consumer and dealer demand equations, only the gasoline price effects on quantities demanded are discussed here. Thus the coefficients on the gasoline variables in the dealer demand equations are relevant for the current discussion. These coefficients and corresponding elasticities are reported in Table 5.5 below.

For Japanese cars, it is evident from Table 5.5 that the positive gasoline price effect dominated the negative. The coefficient of GAS is positive for the period representing the first gasoline price shock and it is positive, although smaller, for the period of the second gasoline price shock. This reduction in size of the coefficient on GAS for Japanese cars could reflect the fact that the relative weight of a Japanese car to a U.S. large car increased during the late 1970's and during the 1980's owing to moderate increases in size of the average Japanese car and to the reduction in size of U.S. large cars.

The variables for gasoline prices were not significantly different from zero in the estimated dealer demand equation for U.S. small cars. This could be the result of the opposing effects of the gasoline price variable being equally as strong. However, as expected, the coefficient on GAS is negative and highly significant for U.S. large cars. Also the positive coefficient on OPEC indicates that size reductions of U.S. large cars in the late 1970's and in the 1980's had a significant effect on the market's perception of the cost of operating those cars.

Table 5.5: Gasoline Price Coefficients and Elasticities

	GAS	
	1973:1 - 1979:3	*1979:4 - 1986:4*
QD1	1481 (0.5)	1035 (0.2)
QD2	0	0
QD3	-17401 (-1.0)	-13768 (-1.4)
Note: Elasticities appear in parentheses.		

In terms of elasticities, for the period 1973:1 to 1979:3, a 1% increase in the price of gasoline caused a 0.5% increase in quantities sold of Japanese cars, but a 1% decrease in quantities sold of U.S. large cars. For the period 1979:4 to 1986:4, the effects on quantities sold caused by a 1% increase in gasoline price were a 0.2% increase for Japanese cars and a 1.4% decrease for U.S. large cars. Thus, although the demand curve for U.S. large cars did not shift as much in response to changes in gasoline prices after the size reductions, the negative response in quantities sold to a change in gasoline price was still greater during the second round of gasoline price increases.

5.4 CONJECTURAL VARIATION PARAMETERS

The behavior of both Japanese and U.S. manufacturers is expected to change with the imposition of quantity restraints. On the one hand, since the Japanese are quantity-constrained because of the VER, then the prices set by U.S. producers should become more relevant to the Japanese producers as they set their prices. Therefore, the CV parameter for U.S. producers, which measures the response of Japanese wholesale prices to a change in the wholesale prices of U.S. producers, should increase under the VER as U.S. producers perceive the increased importance of their price strategies to the realization of any profit maximization goals of the Japanese. On the other hand, since the prevailing price of Japanese cars under the VER should theoretically depend on the price of U.S. cars, then the CV parameter for Japanese producers under the VER is expected to be close to zero. So, if it were positive or negative in the pre-VER period, the CV parameter for the Japanese would be expected to fall or rise, respectively. If it were zero prior to the VER, then no change in that parameter would be expected.

To test these theoretically based predictions, the CV parameters entering the equations are multiplied by dummy variables which allow these parameters to assume different values during the pre-VER period from those they assume during the VER period. Since market behavior is expected gradually to change over time as each manufacturer adjusts to the new price responses of rivals, the dummy variables VER814 and VER846 have been made to interact with the CV parameters. The estimated CV parameters and their corresponding elasticities are presented in Table 5.6 below.

Two conclusions are drawn from the results in Table 5.6. First, prior to the VER, the perceived Japanese price response was zero while the perceived U.S. price response was positive. Stated differently, U.S. producers appeared to assume that Japanese car prices would remain fixed as they chose the profit maximizing wholesale price of their large cars. In contrast, while setting their profit maximizing prices, Japanese producers appeared to expect a price-matching response by U.S. manufacturers. In particular, the conjectural variation elasticity for U.S. manufacturers is -1.9, but not significantly different from zero.[81] Although the conjectural elasticity for the Japanese is smaller (in absolute value) than that for the U.S., it is statistically significant indicating that the Japanese perceived a 8.2% ($636) increase in the wholesale price of U.S. large cars in response to a 10% ($584) increase in their wholesale price. Thus, while purely competitive, Bertrand and collusive behaviors are all rejected by the model's CV estimates, the existence of Japanese price leadership *vis-à-vis* the U.S. producers cannot be rejected for the pre-VER period. This is a surprising result

---

[81]Significance was determined using a two-tailed t-test allowing a 10% level of significance.

Table 5.6: Conjectural Variation Parameters
and Conjectural Variation Elasticities

	1973:1 - 1981:1	*1981:2 - 1984:1*	*1984:2 - 1986:4*
cv_{31}	1.09 (0.82)	0.90 (0.67)	0.49 (0.37)
cv_{13}	-1.43 (-1.90)	-0.22 (-0.30)	-0.31 (-0.42)

Note: The CV elasticities are in parentheses. cv_{31} denotes the Japanese manufacturers' conjecture on the U.S. manufacturers' price response and cv_{13} denotes the U.S. manufacturers' conjecture on the Japanese manufacturers' price response.

since, in terms of market share, U.S. manufacturers were the dominant producers in the domestic market.

Kwoka (1984), however, presents evidence which indicates that Japanese price leadership did exist in the U.S. automobile market during the late 1970's. Although U.S. automobile manufacturers had a significantly higher share of the U.S. market than their Japanese competitors, the Japanese enjoyed a cost advantage *vis-à-vis* the U.S (see Figure 5.1 below). Kwoka therefore argues that U.S. manufacturers followed the profit maximizing strategy of dynamic limit pricing, thereby increasing their prices in response to Japanese price increases and forgoing market share. He finds that between December of 1977 and August of 1978, U.S. producers increased the prices of their small cars in response to the price increases of Japanese cars. The Japanese price increases were caused by the appreciation of the yen against the dollar. Since U.S. producers were following the three-fourths pricing rule discussed earlier in thesis, it is reasonable to assume that U.S. large car prices also followed the upward trend of Japanese car prices. Therefore, at least for that nine-month period, there is evidence of the U.S. producers relinquishing the price leadership role to the Japanese. If U.S. producers were following a

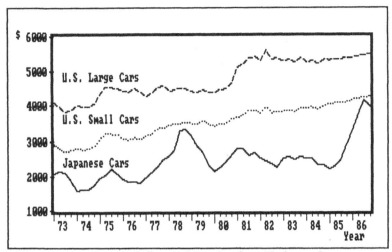

Figure 5.1: Marginal Costs of Production--Estimated
(Denominated in 1982 Dollars)

dynamic limit pricing strategy over the entire pre-VER period because of the Japanese cost advantage, then it is possible for the model to detect price-matching behavior on the part of U.S. producers for that period.

The second of the two conclusions drawn from Table 5.6 is that the perceptions of the U.S. and Japanese manufacturers changed in the direction suggested by the theory. Initially, the reduction in size of the CV parameter for the Japanese manufacturers was insignificant. But, by the late VER period, that parameter had significantly fallen, yielding a conjectural elasticity of 0.37. Thus, Japanese manufacturers would now be expecting a $378 increase in the wholesale price of U.S. large cars (instead of a $838 increase calculated at the pre-VER elasticity value) to accompany a 10% ($762) increase in the wholesale price of Japanese cars. Although the CV parameter for U.S. manufacturers remained significantly close to zero, it did increase in value from its pre-VER level.

These estimates indicate that the VER did have an effect on the behavior of firms in the domestic automobile market.[82] However, a longer period under the VER is needed to determine whether the VER provided an opportunity for U.S. producers to assume a price leadership role in the domestic market. Also, the CV parameters estimated by the model represent average behavior for a given period. To determine whether producers exhibit the same pricing strategy under rising prices as they do under falling prices, two additional dummy variables would have to be interacted with the CV parameters--one representing price increases and the other representing price reductions. Implementing this procedure could potentially make the model intractable. Therefore it was not performed for this study.

In order to verify whether or not the estimated CV parameters accurately reflect the strategic behavior of the automobile producers, a theoretically based model was used to test the consistency of CV parameters.[83] Since (a) the demand curves are linear, (b) the marginal costs are constant with respect to quantities and (c) the conjectural variations do not vary with quantities, then consistent conjectural variations are unique. Furthermore, they are defined by:

$$cv_{ij} \equiv \frac{dW_i(.)}{dW_j}, \text{ for } i \neq j$$

where i represents one manufacturer and j the other. Making substitutions on the right hand side yields:

$$cv_{ij} = \frac{-b_{ii}*b_{jj} + [(b_{ii}*b_{jj})(b_{ii}*b_{jj} - b_{ij}*b_{ji})]^{\frac{1}{2}}}{-b_{ii}*b_{ji}} \tag{17}$$

where i and j are defined as above and b_{ii} and b_{ij} are in absolute value terms. A t-test was used to evaluate the equivalence of the values on

---

[82]It is interesting to note that the U.S. price response during the appreciation of the yen against the dollar during the late VER period was of lesser magnitude than during the same circumstances in the pre-VER period.

[83]A similar procedure was used by Liang (1988) in her investigation of monopoly power in the breakfast cereal industry.

the left and right sides of (17). The respective t-statistics indicate whether each conjecture is consistent.

Since the model does not detect any change in the slopes of the dealer demand curves, only one value is calculated on the right hand side of (17). So unless the model estimates a change in slope of the dealer demand curves during the VER period, the calculated CV parameters will not signify a change in market behavior. Also, the calculation of that value requires the solving of a quadratic equation. Of the two values obtained during this calculation, only the one corresponding to the positive quadratic term yields the reasonable solution.

For the pre-VER period, the calculated CV parameter for the Japanese was 0.39. This suggests that Japanese producers perceived matching behavior on the part of the U.S. producers but not as high a response as the estimated value predicts. The difference between the estimated and calculated CV parameters for the Japanese producers is statistically significant except at the 1% level, given a two-tailed t-test. For U.S. producers, the calculated CV is 0.25, an opposite in sign from the estimated CV. But, while the difference between these two parameters is statistically significant at the 10% level, it is not at the 5% level. Thus, for the period prior to the VER, if the 5% significance level is assumed, the consistency of the Japanese conjecture is rejected, while that of the U.S. manufacturers is accepted.

For the VER period, the test for consistency of the Japanese CV parameter is inconclusive. Since dummy variables for each quarter of that period are included in the dealer demand equation for Japanese cars, the model does not detect changes in the slope of that demand curve. For the U.S., the difference between the estimated and calculated CV parameters is even smaller and thus the difference remains insignificant at the 5% level.

In summary, the estimated CV parameters reveal that Japanese price leadership behavior prevailed before the VER was imposed. A weakening of the Japanese leadership role can be attributed to the VER, although a reversal of roles was not detected possibly because the time horizon used in this study was unavoidably too short. The test for consistency of conjecture reveals an inconsistency in conjecture by the Japanese during the pre-VER period. However, this inconsistency pertains to the strength of the perceived cooperative behavior of U.S. producers and not to the mere existence of that behavior. U.S. producers are shown to take Japanese wholesale prices as given over the entire period of estimation, with some indication of movement toward taking a price leadership role.

5.5 VER EFFECTS ON QUANTITIES, PRICES AND PROFITS

The estimated equations for transaction prices, wholesale prices and quantities are used to simulate values of their endogenous variables for the period 1981:2 to 1986:4. The VER dummy variables are all set equal to zero during the simulation. Thus consumers' preferences for the different types of automobiles and competitive behavior among producers, which existed prior to the VER, are assumed to be relevant for the 1980's without the presence of the VER.

Of the estimated equations used to forecast prices and quantities, the equation for wholesale prices of Japanese cars is the only one in which the Durbin-Watson (DW) statistic indicates significant positive serial correlation among its error terms. The presence of serial correlation of the error terms in that equation therefore results in inaccurate predictions of wholesale prices for Japanese cars. This problem does not bias the CV parameters estimated by that equation. But, it is possible that the level of significance of those parameters could decrease if the serial correlation were removed.

For three stage least squares, there is no program known to this author that corrects for serial correlation of error terms. So an iterative procedure would have to be implemented in which the coefficient of correlation is estimated using two stage least squares. Then, after creating new variables by adjusting the original variables by the correlation coefficient, a generalized least square estimation of the model would have to be performed. But this procedure has its drawbacks. First, it only corrects for first order serial correlation. Second, in a nonlinear system, the accuracy of such corrections is suspect. It is possible that the procedure would have to be performed several times until the correlation coefficient converges to its true value. This could severely curtail the number of degrees of freedom available for estimation. Third, lagged values of the independent variables would have to be included in the list of instruments. This, again, has the potential of limiting the available degrees of freedom. For these reasons, no procedure is utilized during estimation to correct for the correlation of error terms in the Japanese wholesale price equation.

Instead, the cross equation restrictions are removed from all of the manufacturer behavioral equations and VER dummy variables are placed on the marginal cost variable. Removal of the cross equation restrictions from the manufacturer behavioral equations and the inclusion of VER dummy variables on the cost variable might correct the autocorrelation problem for the following reason. In the constrained wholesale price equations, the CV parameters are expected to capture part of the price markup above marginal cost not accounted for by the demand elasticities. In the unconstrained equations, fluctuations in the dependence of price on marginal cost are captured by the reflected differences as the coefficients change with the VER. Since the CV parameters remain constant for a given period of time and marginal cost vary with time, a more pronounced correlation of error terms would be expected to exist within the constrained equations and not in the unconstrained equations. In the wholesale price equation for the Japanese, the VER dummy variables do reflect a change in the dependence of those prices on costs. This could in part be attributed to the fluctuation in the yen-dollar exchange rate. For the unconstrained model, the Durbin-Watson statistic for the Japanese wholesale price equation falls within the critical boundary values for the DW statistic, thus implying that there is no conclusive evidence of positive autocorrelation.

In the wholesale price equation for U.S. large cars, the marginal cost coefficients do not significantly vary with the VER dummy variables. Hence they are omitted from that wholesale price equation. As a result, the DW statistics for the constrained and unconstrained wholesale price equations for U.S. large cars are approximately the same.

The VER is expected to increase domestic prices of U.S. and Japanese cars for five reasons. First, scarcity of Japanese cars leads to excess demands which in turn bid up Japanese car prices. Second, since U.S. cars are substitutes (albeit imperfect) for Japanese cars, some of the demand for Japanese cars is shifted to U.S. cars because of higher Japanese car prices. As U.S. producers face a less price-elastic demand curve in the neighborhood of the former equilibrium prices, they can strategically increase price to the level where the VER is just binding on the Japanese. Third, a second round of Japanese price increases might ensue as the higher U.S. prices acerbate the binding effect of the restraint on the Japanese. Fourth, the estimated conjectural variation parameters for the Japanese suggest that U.S. producers match the price changes of Japanese producers. Therefore, if the Japanese increase their prices with the VER, U.S. producers are expected to follow suit.[84]

The fifth reason for expecting prices to increase is related to increases in product quality. If consumer preferences are increasing in product quality, then a VER-induced increase in quality could shift out the demand curve, thus causing prices to rise. Industry studies show that markups above cost on options can be quite substantial and that profit margins are greater on larger or more luxurious cars than on small economy cars. Thus quality and prices are shown to be positively correlated.

A prediction of the VER's net effect on quantities of U.S. cars sold is based on the own- and cross-price elasticities of demand. Since the own-price elasticity of demand for U.S. large cars is negative, through the own-price elasticity effect, the VER is expected to have a negative influence on quantities sold of U.S. large cars. However, the cross-price elasticity of demand for U.S. large cars with respect to the price of Japanese cars is positive. Hence, an increase in the wholesale price of Japanese cars, attributable to the VER, is expected to have a positive influence on quantities sold of U.S. large cars, given the Japanese price effect. Since the own-price elasticity is greater than the cross-price elasticity, then if wholesale prices of Japanese cars increase by the same percentage or by a smaller percentage than those for U.S. large cars, the VER is expected to have a negative effect on quantities sold of U.S. large cars. If the percentage increase in wholesale prices of Japanese cars is sufficiently high compared to those for U.S. large cars, then the VER could have a positive effect on quantities sold of U.S. large cars. Thus, *a priori*, no definite prediction can be made as

---

[84]Krishna (1987) refers to the first three reasons as the competitive, monopoly and interactive effects, respectively. Note that these changes represent only partial effects of the VER in the neighborhood of the initial equilibrium. As stated earlier, the final outcome with respect to quantities depends on the changes in all prices. Thus the demand elasticities calculated for U.S. large cars are more elastic for the VER period than for the pre-VER period.

to the VER's effects on the number of U.S. large cars sold. If quantities of both Japanese and U.S. cars are lower under the VER than they otherwise would have been, then the VER is expected to have a positive impact on transaction prices of all cars sold in the domestic market.

Review of previous studies also yields mixed results with respect to quantities. Willig and Dutz (1987) calculate an increase in U.S. quantities, while Mannering and Winston (1987) estimate a decrease. Since the predicted VER effects on prices hinge on the degree to which the quantity restraint is binding, discussion on the quantity effects precedes that on the price effects. A summary of the estimated VER effects on quantities is presented in Table 5.7 at the end of this chapter.

It is no surprise that the Japanese sold fewer cars in the U.S. market with than without the VER. However, it is important to determine how many more Japanese cars would have been imported without the quantity restriction. Although quantities sold of Japanese cars increased in every year excepting 1981,[85] the Japanese could still have sold approximately 1.7 million (15%) more cars over the VER period if the restraint had not been implemented. The incidence of the VER appeared to be higher between 1984 and 1986 owing to the economic expansion in the U.S. Since demand for Japanese cars is positively related to real income and negatively related to lagged values of the unemployment rate, rising income and falling unemployment during the late period of the VER would lead to a higher number of Japanese cars sold than allowed by the quota restriction.[86] The

---

[85]For the first four quarters after the VER was imposed (1981:2 to 1982:1), quantities sold of Japanese cars were 0.05% below the level in the four quarters prior to the VER (1980:2 to 1981:1). In subsequent years, quantities increased by .04%, .06%, .03% and .17%.

[86]During the late VER period, gasoline prices had begun to fall. Since gasoline prices had a positive coefficient in the dealer demand equation for Japanese cars, the gasoline price effect would cause an inward shift of the demand curve for Japanese cars. Therefore, the strength of Japanese car sales (with or without the VER) in the late VER period is attributed to the U.S. having a strong economy.

restraint was therefore still binding during the late VER period even though the Japanese twice raised the quota levels during that period.

Instead of seizing the opportunity to fill the void created by the temporary retreat of the Japanese, U.S. producers actually sold fewer cars under the VER than they otherwise would have. The model predicts that U.S. manufacturers sold 6.3 million (15.4%) fewer cars under the VER than they would have if the restraint had not been imposed. These quantity reductions are totally attributed to the VER. Since the demand equations for U.S. small and large cars include variables which represent the overall strength of the national economy (such as real income, consumer sentiment index and unemployment rate), the number of cars sold without the influence of the VER are simulated under the same economic conditions which prevailed during the VER. The simulation results show that, between 1981 and 1984, almost 1 million more U.S. large cars would have been sold without the VER, even though the U.S. was experiencing an economic recession. For the entire VER period, 3.6 million (16%) fewer U.S. large cars were domestically sold.

During the period of economic recession, the number of U.S. small cars sold was 2 million fewer than what would have been sold without the VER. Purchases of these cars were affected by the VER in two ways. First, a significant number of U.S. small cars were captive imports made in Japan and therefore were included in the VER. This effect is evidenced by the fact that twice as many U.S. small car than large car sales were foregone during the early VER period. Second, as with the large cars, the fall in purchases of U.S. small cars was caused by increases in their prices. Since the estimated demand elasticities for U.S. small cars are not significantly different from zero, the limited availability of captive imports is probably the main cause of the reduction in sales of U.S. small cars. In total, during the entire VER period, 2.7 (14.8%) million more U.S. small cars could have been sold in the absence of the restraint. It can therefore be deduced that U.S. automobile workers did not receive the expected increase in employment from the VER.

The reduction in quantities of U.S. and Japanese cars was accompanied by higher wholesale and transaction prices. The model predicts that wholesale prices of U.S. cars would be significantly higher during the 1980's than if the VER had not been imposed. What is more, the model predicts that the VER would have a much greater impact on U.S. cars than it would have on Japanese cars. These effects are even more exaggerated for transaction prices. A summary of the changes in wholesale and transaction prices caused by the VER is reported in Tables 5.7 at the end of this chapter. All prices reported below and in the table are denominated in 1982 dollars.

For the early VER period, wholesale prices of U.S. large cars were (on average) $655 (7.8%) higher than they would have been without the VER. Instead of the 17.7% wholesale price increase from the pre-VER to the early period, prices would have increased by 9.3% without the VER.[87] Thus 8.4% of the price increase from the pre-VER period to the early VER period can be attributed to VER. For the late VER period, the average wholesale price for U.S. large cars was $872 (9.3%) higher because of the VER. There would have been a 9.8% instead of a 11.5% increase in wholesale prices of U.S. large cars from the early to the late VER period if the VER had not been imposed.[88] These relatively large increases in prices with or without the VER during the late VER period are probably the result of stronger demand during the economic recovery.

Not surprisingly, a similar pattern of wholesale price increases is seen for U.S. small cars. Wholesale prices of these cars were $334 (5.2%) higher in the early VER period and $451 (6.6%) higher in the late VER period because of the VER. Between the pre-VER and early VER periods, there was a 12.9% increase in these prices. But without the VER, there would only have been a 7.4% increase. Thus, 5.5% of the actual increase can be attributed to the VER for the early VER period. For the late VER period, the actual increase from the early VER period in wholesale prices of U.S. small cars was 7.8%, while the model predicted an increase of 6.5% without the VER.

The increase in the wholesale prices of Japanese cars predicted by the model are significantly lower than those for U.S. cars over the entire VER period. For the early VER period, the average difference

---

[87]The 9.3% estimate is the percentage change in wholesale price of U.S. large cars from the pre-VER period to the early VER period without the VER, the latter price being estimated by subtracting $670 from the average price for that period.

[88]Since the same value for the early VER period is not used for the calculations, the 1.7% difference does not measure the influence of the VER in the late VER period.

between actual and predicted wholesale prices of Japanese cars is $342 (5.3%). Calculations based on this estimate indicates that, of the 14% increase in wholesale prices of Japanese cars that occurred between the pre-VER and early VER periods, 5.7% can be attributed to the VER. In other words, 8.3% of the increase in wholesale prices of Japanese cars between the two periods would have occurred without the VER. The model's predictions for the late VER period indicate that Japanese wholesale prices were (on average) $74 (0.9%) lower with than without the VER. This is, however, an insignificant difference given the error of prediction inherent in forecasting models.[89] For 1986, predicted values exceeded actual values by $410. Between the early and late VER periods, the actual wholesale prices of Japanese cars increased by 13.2%, but there would have been an estimated 20.4% increase in these prices without the VER.

This result is somewhat surprising since it was expected that wholesale VER prices of Japanese cars would be higher than they would have been without the VER as long as this restraint was binding. The model predicts that the late VER period would be the period during which this restraint would be most severely binding. However, examination of the coefficients for that equation in the unrestricted model reveals strong negative relationships between the wholesale price of Japanese cars and two of its explanatory variables for the late VER period: marginal cost in dollar terms and wholesale price of U.S. large cars. These negative coefficients perform the same duty as the negative coefficient on the CV parameter in the alternative model for the late VER period. Thus, when the VER dummy variables are set to zero, predicted values of the Japanese wholesale prices for the late VER period rise faster than they would have under the restraint.

In percentage terms, the increases in transaction prices of U.S. large cars attributable to the VER are significantly higher than the corresponding increases in their wholesale prices. During the early

---

[89]Confidence intervals are not calculated for any of the model's predictions since the model is nonlinear in its parameters. Only by choosing a large number of alternative values for each estimated coefficient while performing simulations can such intervals be established. This procedure was not deemed practical for this study because the model estimates too many coefficients for such an application to be feasible.

VER period, actual transaction prices of U.S. large cars exceed their predicted values by an average of $1,036 (10.4%). Comparison of transaction prices for the pre-VER and early VER periods reveals a 15% increase with the VER effects and a 4.3% increase without them. Hence, 10.7% of the increase in prices between periods is attributable to the VER. In the late VER period, transaction prices of U.S. large cars were (on average) $1,339 (12.8%) higher than they would have been had the VER not been imposed. While transaction prices actually increased by 5.7% during this period, the estimated increase without the VER would have been 3.3%. Thus, although the VER had a greater positive impact on transaction prices than on wholesale prices of U.S. large cars, the increases between periods for transaction prices were smaller than those for wholesale prices.

During the early VER period, the average increase in transaction price of U.S. small cars which can be attributed to the restriction is $467 (6.4%). The corresponding increase for the late VER period is $433 (6.1%), a slightly more moderate increase than in the previous period. Between the pre-VER and early VER periods, transaction prices of U.S. small cars actually increased by 12.1%. However, the model predicts a smaller increase of 5.3% without the influence of the VER. Transaction prices actually decreased by 2.6% for U.S. small cars between the early and late VER periods. If the VER had not been imposed, these transaction prices would have still decreased by approximately 2.3%. Interestingly enough, there is a wider gap between wholesale and transaction prices of U.S. cars during the 1980's because of the VER. There is also a wider gap between changes in prices of these cars at the retail level than at the wholesale level. This is consistent with the fact that U.S. producers pegged the wholesale prices of U.S. small cars to those of U.S. large cars, while consumers had a valuation of the two cars which did not coincide with that of the producers.

Ironically, domestic dealers of U.S. cars took greater advantage of the VER to raise their prices than did domestic dealers of Japanese cars. For the early VER period, the model predicts that transaction prices of Japanese cars would be only $228 (2.9%) above what they would have been in the absence of VER. Comparison of these transaction prices for the pre- and early VER periods reveals that prices increased by 12.9% and 9.7% with and without the VER, respectively. These simulations reveal little influence of the VER over transaction prices during the early VER period.

For the late VER period, there was a larger effect of the restraint on transaction prices of Japanese cars. Specifically, the model predicts that transaction prices would be $533 (5.8%) higher during that period than if the VER had not been imposed. Between the early and late VER periods, transaction prices actually increased by 17.2%, while, without the VER, they would have increased by 13.8%.

A surprising result is that, although the VER was binding during the entire period of the simulation, for the entire VER period, U.S. producers priced more aggressively than Japanese producers. It is also clear that domestic dealers of Japanese cars did not initially take advantage of the VER to inflate their prices. One possible reason for the moderate price response of the Japanese is that they might have had dual objectives: maximizing profits, while maintaining or increasing market share. This could otherwise be stated as an intertemporal profit maximization problem. As noted earlier, since the VER was imposed during the economic recession of the early 1980's, demand for automobiles in the domestic market was slack. Thus, curtailing exports to the U.S. during that period did not present severe limitations on the quantities Japanese producers could sell in the U.S. market.

This idea is borne out by the relatively low reductions in quantities sold of Japanese and U.S. large cars during that period. However, when the VER was more severely binding (the late VER period), Japanese producers could have restrained increases in the wholesale prices of their cars in attempt to maintain their customer base. If prices were kept relatively low, domestic consumers of Japanese cars attempting to replace their present car would probably still order a Japanese car and wait for it to arrive at the dealership. Such behavior is well documented in newspapers and trade press for the years 1984 through 1986.

Because of the weak market for cars in the early 1980's, domestic dealers of Japanese cars could not enforce large price increases and still maximize profits. Hence, this largely explains why the VER had only a small positive price effect on the Japanese during the early VER period. However, with economic recovery and the coincident strengthening of the demand for cars in the U.S. market, domestic dealers of Japanese cars could charge premiums above the manufacturer's suggested retail price (MSRP) and still sell their full restricted supply of cars. Thus the model's predictions on quantities and prices are deemed consistent with actual occurrences during the period of the VER.

But, in order to gauge which manufacturers and dealers gained or incurred losses because of the VER, the VER's effects on profits are now analyzed. Gains or loses to manufacturers and dealers which are attributed to the VER can simply be calculated from:

$$\Pi^F = (W_i * QD_i - \hat{W}_i * \hat{QD}_i) - MC_i * (QD_i - \hat{QD}_i)$$

$$\Pi^D = (P_i * QD_i - \hat{P}_i * \hat{QD}_i) - [(W_i + S) * QD_i - (\hat{W}_i + S) * \hat{QD}_i]$$

where $\hat{P}_i$, $\hat{W}_i$ and $\hat{QD}_i$ are the predicted values of transaction prices, wholesale prices and quantities, respectively, without the VER. The marginal cost estimates are not affected by the VER since they are assumed to be constant with respect to quantities, and since manufacturers are assumed to be price takers in input markets. It has been assumed that the input market is perfectly competitive. However, if the markets for labor, intermediate products, raw materials or capital are imperfectly competitive, then the suppliers in those markets could bid away some of the VER-generated profits earned by automobile manufacturers. Thus, the greater the degree of monopoly power exercised by input suppliers, the more will the present model overestimate the VER's benefits to automobile producers.

In Table 5.7 at the end of this chapter, a summary of the changes in manufacturer and dealer profits (denominated in 1982 dollars) attributable to the VER is presented. From these estimates, three significant conclusions can be drawn as to the VER's effects on profits in the domestic automobile market: (1) U.S. manufacturers gain while Japanese manufacturers lose; (2) all domestic dealers gain, with U.S. car dealers gaining more than domestic Japanese car dealers; (3) dealers gain more than manufacturers.

With respect to the first conclusion, for the entire VER period, profits of U.S. automobile manufacturers were $3.93 billion greater than they would have been had the VER not been imposed. The Japanese manufacturers incurred an estimated $6.15 billion in profit reductions owing to the VER. This result is startling considering that the VER is "voluntary" and that the Japanese continue to renew the restriction even to the present.

However, if the Japanese were indeed following a long term profit maximizing strategy as well as endeavoring to maintain market share in the U.S., it is possible that these profits were foregone with a view to earning higher profits in the future. It is also possible that the

Japanese chose to limit exports to the U.S. voluntarily instead of facing more harmful trade restrictions on cars or on other products. For example, in 1980 the United Auto Workers proposed a local content rule which would require the vehicles sold in the U.S. by foreign manufacturers to be comprised of 80% of U.S. made parts by 1983. At the same time, the Mottl bill was proposed which would limit imports of cars and trucks to a 10% domestic market share for a five year period.[90] In 1981 the Danforth-Bentson bill also proposed mandatory quotas.[91] Tariff restrictions on Japanese cars were even being considered in 1985.[92] Any one of these proposed limits on imported Japanese cars could have reduced Japanese profits by more than the VER.

U.S. producers appeared to gain in all years except for 1981. During that year, sharp reductions in quantities sold of U.S. large cars and moderate increases in their wholesale prices (compared to their increases in subsequent years) account for the losses of $0.26 billion in the large car category which could be attributed to the VER. Losses of $0.59 in the U.S. small cars category bring total losses in 1981 to $0.85 billion for U.S. manufacturers. In subsequent years, profits for U.S. large cars were positive except for 1986. In that year, very large reductions in quantities sold were not compensated for by the significantly higher wholesale prices under the VER. For that year, however, U.S. small cars earned enough profits to make the total effect of the VER a positive $0.7 billion. It was only in the last two years that profits of U.S. small cars were positively affected by the VER.

The only year in which the VER had a positive effect on the profits of Japanese manufacturers was the year in which the VER was least binding. In 1983, the VER's effect on quantities of Japanese cars sold domestically was the smallest, while the effect on wholesale prices was the largest for the entire VER period. Thus Japanese manufacturers gained an estimated total of $0.41 billion in 1983 because of the VER. It is interesting to note that U.S. manufacturers benefitted the most

---

[90]See United States Congress, Joint Economic Committee (1980), p. 137.

[91]See United States, Committee on Ways and Means (1985), p.267.

[92]See J. S. Power and Associates (1985), p. 2.

from the VER in that same year. The year in which the VER had its most damaging effect on Japanese manufacturers' profits was 1986. For that year, the model predicts that the VER was most severely binding and that wholesale prices of Japanese cars would have been higher without the VER. Data on subsequent years would have to be analyzed in order to determine whether or not these negative effects on Japanese manufacturers' profits persisted.

The model predicts that domestic dealers of U.S. cars would gain significantly as a result of the VER. Although dealers of U.S. cars made marginal gains and sometimes incurred losses on their small cars, U.S. large car profits were always higher than they would have been without the VER. Specifically, U.S. dealers earned an estimated $6.68 billion on their large cars over the entire VER period which can be attributed to the VER. Their highest gains were made in 1986, the year in which the VER had its largest negative effect on profits of U.S. manufacturers. With respect to U.S. small cars, gains attributed to the VER were $0.25 billion over the entire VER period. The two years, 1983 and 1986, for which dealers of U.S. cars experienced their highest gains from the VER in the large car category are the same years in which the VER's effect on their profits from U.S. small cars was negative. Even though the VER's impact on profits for U.S. small cars was negative in those years, in no year did the model predict an overall loss for dealers of U.S. cars. In total, dealers of U.S. cars earned an estimated $6.93 billion dollars over the entire VER period.

In contrast, only $1.40 billion of the profits earned by domestic dealers of Japanese cars can be attributed to the VER. In 1982 through 1984, these dealers actually earned less than they would have, had the VER not been imposed. By the model's estimates, the negative effect reported for 1982 is approximately 6% of dealer profits for that year. This is an insignificant change compared to the 60% and 65% reductions estimated for 1983 and 1984, respectively. In those two year, the differences between actual and predicted transaction prices were not significant. Also, wholesale price increases for Japanese cars attributable to the VER were their greatest in those years. Thus, with the reduction in quantities attributed to the restriction, profits at the dealer level on Japanese cars were adversely affected by the VER.

Over the entire VER period, domestic automobile dealers earned a total of $8.33 billion more than they would have earned without the VER. The VER induced an estimated $2.22 billion decrease in the combined profits of U.S. and Japanese manufacturers. Domestic dealers of U.S. cars benefitted more from the VER than did manufacturers of U.S. cars. However, while domestic dealers of Japanese cars reaped modest gains, the manufacturers of Japanese cars for the domestic market incurred significant losses because of the VER. Thus, with respect to national welfare, the model predicts a positive impact of $12.26 billion, considering *only* the VER's effects on profits of domestic dealers and of U.S. manufacturers.

In summary, the model predicts that the VER transferred surplus value from domestic consumers and Japanese automobile manufacturers to U.S. automobile manufacturers and domestic dealers of both U.S. and Japanese cars. VER induced profits from selling Japanese cars in the domestic market were earned only by domestic dealers. These gains were small in comparison to the profit reductions experienced by Japanese manufacturers and in comparison to the gains earned by domestic dealers of U.S. cars. The biggest winners overall were the domestic dealers.

Table 5.7: VER's Effects on Quantities, Prices and Profits

	Early VER Period	Late VER Period	Full VER Period
Quantities ($mill.)			
Japanese	-0.6	-1.1	-1.7
U.S.	-3.1	-3.2	-6.3
small	-2.1	-0.6	-2.7
large	-1.0	-2.6	-3.6
Wholesale Prices ($1982)			
Japanese	+ 342	- 74	+ 98
U.S.			
small	+ 334	+ 451	+ 412
large	+ 655	+ 872	+ 756
Transaction Prices ($1982)			
Japanese	+ 228	+ 533	+ 370
U.S.			
small	+ 467	+ 433	+ 442
large	+1036	+1339	+1195
Manufacturer Profits ($bill.)			
Japanese	- 0.36	- 5.79	- 6.15
U.S.	- 0.70	+3.23	+3.93
small	- 2.71	+2.60	- 0.11
large	+3.41	+0.63	+4.04
Dealer Profits ($bill.)			
Japanese	- 1.24	+2.64	+1.40
U.S.	+2.82	+4.11	+6.93
small	+0.26	- 0.01	+0.25
large	+2.56	+4.12	+6.68

6.0 Conclusion

6.1 SUMMARY REMARKS

For almost a decade now, researchers have been using theoretical and empirical models to assess the impact of the VER on national welfare. However, each of those models has limitations which impede its ability accurately to measure the VER's effects. For example, recent studies compare predicted prices and quantities to their pre-VER values in order to obtain estimates of the VER's welfare impact. This procedure assumes that without the VER, prices and quantities would have remained at their pre-VER levels. Therefore the longer the forecast horizon, the less accurate would be the measurement of the welfare effect. More recent studies correct this problem by comparing actual values of prices and quantities to their predicted values without the influence of the VER. However, those studies make inappropriate use of previously estimated demand elasticities or of previously formulated assumptions regarding market behavior. What is more, in assessing the VER's effects on national welfare, none of these studies accounts for the profits earned or losses incurred by domestic dealers of Japanese cars which should be entered as an adjustment to national welfare. This study, therefore, has undertaken the dual purpose of evaluating the change in market rivalry between Japanese and U.S. producers with the imposition of the VER and of assessing the VER's impact on profits of Japanese and U.S. automobile manufacturers and their domestic dealers, while eschewing the pitfalls of earlier studies.

From 1973 up to the imposition of the VER in 1981, the model rejects the Bertrand and collusive behavior between Japanese and U.S. producers in the domestic automobile market, suggesting instead that the Japanese were price leaders *vis-à-vis* the U.S. producers. The Japanese perception of the U.S. price response has been found to be consistent with matching behavior, while the U.S. perception of the Japanese price response is insignificant. This is indeed a surprising result since, during that period, U.S. producers maintained a large share of the market. However, calculated estimates of the respective consistent conjectures do not contradict this finding. This result therefore supports Crandall's assumption of Japanese price leadership when he formulated his U.S. price equations.

The change in the conjectural variation parameters from the pre-VER to the VER period is consistent with a move toward U.S. price leadership. But, more conclusive evidence of a change in pricing strategies would require simulation over a longer VER period. These results do suggest, however, that Crandall's estimate of the conjectural elasticity for U.S. producers does not purely reflect the behavioral response of those producers prior to the VER. Therefore Crandall (and thus Mannering and Winston) is likely to over estimate the difference between actual and predicted prices of U.S. cars.

The behavioral assumptions for the pre-VER period do have some bearing on the simulated values of prices and quantities. For example, if Bertrand behavior is posited *a priori*, the CV parameters would be set to zero. Given that the estimated CV parameter for Japanese producers is significantly different from zero, simulated wholesale prices under the two behavioral assumptions would differ. Since these wholesale prices in part determine quantities and quantities in part determine transaction prices, an incorrect assumption about the pricing strategies of the automobile producers prior to the VER could have a significant effect on the evaluation of profits earned by those manufacturers and domestic dealer. The welfare predictions of Tarr and Morkre who assume competitive behavior on behalf of Japanese and U.S. automobile manufacturers are therefore questionable.

Apart from influencing the pricing strategies of the Japanese and U.S. producers, the VER also had a more direct impact on prices and quantities through the scarcity effect. Consistent with previous empirical studies, this model finds that the prices of Japanese and U.S. cars were higher under the VER than they would have been if the VER had not been imposed. However, previous studies did not separately analyze the effects on wholesale and retail prices. Comparison of U.S. large car and Japanese car prices reveals that, for the entire VER period, dealers of U.S. large cars took greater advantage of the VER to increase their transaction prices than did dealers Japanese cars. Similarly, VER-induced increases in wholesale prices of U.S. large cars were consistently greater than those for Japanese cars during the VER period. Model simulation also reveals that dealers of U.S. large cars increased their prices by more than the increases they faced at the wholesale level. For U.S. small cars and Japanese cars, the VER-induced increases in transaction price did not always exceed the related increases in wholesale prices. Thus it can be concluded that the VER marked the critical point at which U.S. manufacturers and their dealers were able to institute significant increases in wholesale and transaction prices.

With regard to quantities, the model joins Mannering and Winston in predicting a reduction in quantities sold of U.S. cars because of the VER. The estimate obtained here is, however, almost 4½ times as large as the Mannering and Winston estimate. Both models arrive at similar estimates of the amount of Japanese cars not domestically sold because of the VER.

It appears that the profit-maximizing strategy of the U.S. manufacturers and their dealers was to implement significant increases in prices while accepting reductions in quantities sold. This strategy reaped for these producers and dealers profit increases of almost $11 billion (in 1982 dollars) from 1981 through 1986. However, contrary to the findings of previous models, Japanese manufacturers incurred losses of approximately $6 billion (in 1982 dollars) over that same period. Higher profits were earned on Japanese cars only at the dealer level. This, again, is a surprising result since the results of previous studies supported the argument that Japanese government extended the VER beyond its initial three year limit because Japanese automobile manufacturers were earning higher profits than they would have earned if the VER were not in effect. The findings of this study suggest that the Japanese might have had alternative reasons for continuing the VER.

One such reason might be that the Japanese trade ministry could have surmised that the U.S. would impose even more odious trade restrictions on Japanese cars or even on other Japanese exports if the Japanese had not continued to limit their exports to the U.S. for an extended period. In addition Japanese automobile manufacturers might have been following a long-run profit maximizing strategy which in part relied on increasing market share over time. In that case they would not find it optimal to gouge on prices in effort to earn high short-run profits while foregoing even higher long-run profits.

Contrary to previous reports, this study finds no evidence of a transfer of surplus from domestic automobile consumers to Japanese automobile producers. Instead, the losses incurred by domestic consumers (see Appendix IV) as a result of the imposition of the VER were captured by U.S. automobile manufacturers and by domestic dealers of U.S. and Japanese cars. Because of increased profits, the VER's net welfare effect was calculated to be over $6 billion (in 1982 dollars). U.S. automobile manufacturers earned all, and possibly more, than they had expected. But, because quantities sold of U.S. cars were lower than they would have been under the VER, it is unlikely that automobile workers got their anticipated 900,000 increase in jobs. It is possible that through bargaining with the automobile producers, labor reaped benefits from the VER in the form of higher wages.

6.2 FUTURE RESEARCH

Given the current framework, the demand-supply model of the domestic automobile industry developed for this thesis can be employed to answer questions pertaining to pricing strategies of Japanese and U.S. automobile producers and to the effects of changes in trade and domestic policies on the market equilibrium and on national welfare. With some adjustments to the model's framework and the gathering of more data, even greater understanding can be obtained of the type of behavior exhibited by individual automobile producers and of the welfare incidence of different economic policies. Four extensions of the current research which should be pursued are described here.

First, the current examination of pricing strategies in the automobile industry under different trade regimes sought to discern the type of market behavior that existed before and during the VER given the prices which prevailed. However, the model can be used to predict the prices and quantities which would prevail given a specified type of market behavior. The simulated prices would be compared to actual prices, thereby indicating the extent to which the levels of automobile prices are influenced by the pricing strategies followed by the automobile producers. Likewise, a comparison of quantities would reveal the effect of market behavior on the domestic market shares of Japanese and U.S. producers.

Second, the structure of the model developed for this study only facilitates examination of the competitive behavior between Japanese and U.S. producers as cooperative groups and therefore prevents the assessment of intra-industry rivalry. Since the data on prices, quantities and costs are available at the firm level, it is possible to develop a more disaggregated model which estimates the pattern of behavior between firms of the same industry. Observing such behavior for the pre-VER and VER periods should reveal whether the quantity restraint leads to more or less collusive behavior among producers in Japanese or U.S. automobile industries.

Third, in model estimation, input prices and output quantities did not adequately explain demand for labor in either the Japanese or the U.S. automobile industry. It is evident that important explanatory variables were excluded from the labor equations or that the functional form of those equations was inappropriate. Improving the specification of the labor equations would serve two purposes. First, including these equations in the estimated model should improve the model's marginal cost estimates since the input demand equations are used to impose cross equation restrictions on the parameters of the cost equations. Second, the VER's impact on employment in the Japanese and U.S. automobile industries would be directly determined through model simulation. Thus another aspect of the VER's effect on domestic welfare could be addressed.

Fourth, some of the current literature on exchange rates focuses on the degree to which fluctuations in a bilateral exchange rate are encountered by the consumer as changes in prices. Since the exchange rate enters the model as an explanatory variable, the degree to which fluctuations in the exchange rate are "passed through" to the consumer as changes in transaction prices of Japanese cars during the pre-VER and VER periods can be estimated.

Appendix I: Segmentation of Car Models

JAPANESE CARS

Datsun/Nissan: B210, F10, Maxima, Pulsar, Pulsar NX, Sentra, Sentra
Transplant, Stanza, 200SX, 210, 240Z, 260Z, 280Z, 280ZX,
300ZX, 310, 311, 510, 610, 710, 810, 1200, Other Models,
Hawaiian Sales;

Honda: Accord, Civic, Civic CRX, N600/Z600, Prelude, Transplant
Honda;

Isuzu: I-Mark, I-Mark (diesel), Impulse;

Mazda: Cosmo, GLC, Miser, RX-2, RX-3, RX-4, RX-7, 323, 626,
1300/808, 1600/800, Other Models;

Mitsubishi: Cordia, Galant, Mirage, Starion, Tredia;

Subaru

Toyota: Camry, Carina, Celica, Corolla, Corolla (NUMMI), Corona,
Cressida, Crown, MR-2, Mark II, Starlet, Supra, Tercel, Other
Models, Hawaiian Sales;

U.S. SMALL CARS

American Motors: AMX, Aliance, Concord, Eagle, Eagle SX4,
Encore, Gremlin, Hornet, Javelin, Pacer, Spirit;

Buick: Apollo, Skyhawk, Skyhawk J, Skylark, Somerset;

Chevrolet: Camaro, Cavalier, Chevette, Citation, Corsica, Monza, Nova, Nova (NUMMI), Spectrum (captive), Sprint (captive), Vega;

Chrysler: Conquest (captive), Laser;

Dodge: Aries, Aspen, challenger, Challenger (captive), Charger '83, Colt (captive), Dart, Daytona, Omni, Omni O24, Shadow, Vista (captive);

Ford: EXP, Escort, Fairmont, Falcon, Granada, Maverick, Mustang, Mustang II, Mustang III, Pinto, Tempo;

Mercury: Bobcat, Capri, Comet, LN7, Lynx, Monarch, Topaz;

Oldsmobile: Calais, Firenza, Omega, Starfire;

Plymouth: Arrow (captive), Barracuda, Champ (captive), Colt (captive), Conquest (captive), Cricket (captive), Horizon, Horizon TC-3, Reliant, Sopporo (captive), Sundance, Turismo, Valiant, Vista (captive), Volare;

Pontiac: Astre, Fiero, Firebird, Grand Am, J-2000, Phoenix, Sunbird, T-1000, Ventura.

U.S. LARGE CARS

American Motors: Ambassador, Matador, Rebel;

Buick: Buick, Century, Century FWD, Electra FWD, LeSabre, Regal, Regal Coupe, Regal Sedan, Riviera;

Cadillac: Cadillac, Cimarron, Eldorado, Seville;

Chevrolet: Celebrity, chevelle, Chevrolet, Corvette, Malibu, Monte Carlo;

Chrysler: Chrysler, Cordoba, E-Class, Imperial, LeBaron, LeBaron K, LeBaron GTS, LeBaron J, New Yorker E, New Yorker 5th Ave.;

Dodge: Charger, Charger SE, Coronet, Diplomat, Dodge 400, Dodge 600, Lancer, Magnum, Mirada, Monaco, Polara, Royal Monaco, St. Regis;

Ford: Crown Victoria, Elite, Fairlane, Ford, LTD II, LTD '83, Taurus, Thunderbird, Torino;

Lincoln: Continental, Lincoln, Mark Series, Versailles;

Mercury: Cougar, Cougar XR-7, Cougar '83, Grand Marquis, Marquis, Mercury, Montego, Sable;

Oldsmobile: Ciera, Cutlass, F-85, Olds 88, Olds 98, Supreme, Toronado;

Plymouth: Belvedere, Caravelle, Fury, Grand Fury, Satellite;

Pontiac: A-6000, Bonneville G, Bonneville H, Grand Prix, LeMans, Parisienne, Pontiac, Tempest.

Appendix II: Japanese and U.S. Makes
Included in Transaction Prices

Japanese	U.S.
Honda import	Buick compact
Honda sub-compact	Buick intermediate
Honda compact	Buick full size
Mazda import	Buick luxury
Mazda sub-compact	Cadillac luxury
Mazda compact	Chevrolet sub-compact
Nissan import	Chevrolet compact
Nissan sub-compact	Chevrolet intermediate
Nissan compact	Chevrolet full size
Nissan intermediate	Chrysler intermediate
Nissan luxury or status	Dodge sub-compact
Subaru import	Dodge compact
Toyota import	Ford sub-compact
Toyota sub-compact	Ford compact
Toyota compact	Ford intermediate
Toyota intermediate	Ford full size
Toyota luxury or status	Mercury sub-compact
	Mercury intermediate
	Mercury full size
	Oldsmobile compact
	Oldsmobile intermediate
	Oldsmobile full size
	Oldsmobile luxury
	Plymouth sub-compact
	Plymouth compact
	Pontiac sub-compact
	Pontiac compact
	Pontiac intermediate

Appendix III: Estimated Equations

VARIABLE LIST

Variables	Description
C	Constant
P(i)	Transaction price of Japanese, U.S. small or U.S. large cars
QD(i)	Quantities demanded of Japanese, U.S. small or U.S. large cars
QD(i)814	Quantities demanded of Japanese, U.S. small or U.S. large cars multiplied by VER814
QD(i)846	Quantities demanded of Japanese, U.S. small or U.S. large cars multiplied by VER846
WS(i)82	Wholesale price of Japanese, U.S. small or U.S. large cars plus cost of selling a car at the dealership
W(i)814	Wholesale price of Japanese, U.S. small or U.S. large cars multiplied by VER814
W(i)846	Wholesale price of Japanese, U.S. small or U.S. large cars multiplied by VER846
YD82	Real income, 1982 dollars
GAS82	Real gasoline price indexes, 1982 base year
OPEC2	GAS82 multiplied by gasoline price dummy variable for 1979:4 to 1986:4
CSI(-n)	Consumer Sentiment Index lagged n periods
CSICH(-n)	Change in CSI lagged n periods
UN(-n)	Unemployment rate lagged n periods
UNCH(-n)	Change in UN lagged n periods
DUM(n)	Quarterly dummy variable for period n
DUM74	Dummy variable for U.S. price adjustment in 1974
T	Time trend
VER814	VER dummy for early VER period, 1981:2 to 1984:1
VER846	VER dummy for late VER period, 1984:2 to 1986:4
JPMC	Marginal cost of Japanese cars in yen
USLMC	Marginal cost of U.S. large cars in dollars
YDOL	Yen-dollar exchange rate
CV31n	Conjectural variation parameter for Japanese manufacturers, n = 0, 1, 2 for pre-VER, early VER and late VER periods, respectively
CV13n	Conjectural variation parameter for U.S. manufacturers, n =

ESTIMATED EQUATIONS

	Full Model	Alternative Model	Unconstrained Model
Dependent Variable: P1	SER: 156.98 DW: 2.0378	SER: 156.21 DW: 2.0938	SER: 158.09 DW: 2.0797
Independent Variables:			
CONSTANT	-3948.20*** (784.36)	-3868.80*** (791.68)	-3932.40*** (767.40)
QD1	-0.003546*** (0.000529)	-0.003447*** (0.000528)	-0.003522*** (0.000507)
QD1814	0.002697** (0.000603)	0.002595*** (0.0006006)	0.002671*** (0.0005939)
QD1846	0.00629*** (0.0008517)	0.006277*** (0.0008618)	0.006419*** (0.0008412)
QD2	-0.0001882 (0.0002587)	-0.0002114 (0.0002608)	-0.0002812 (0.0002501)
QD3	-0.000448*** (0.0001481)	-0.0004519*** (0.0001475)	-0.0004509** (0.000142)
QD3814	-0.001404*** (0.0003118)	-0.00136*** (0.0003114)	-0.001412*** (0.0003063)
YD82	6.9373*** (0.38367)	6.9118*** (0.3894)	6.9012*** (0.3783)
GAS82	-9.5337*** (2.806)	-10.006*** (2.8182)	-9.1628*** (2.7474)
CSI(-2)	-1054.00*** (277.73)	-1047.00*** (279.33)	-924.16*** (271.16)
DUM3	-93.426** (44.410)	-86.641** (44.580)	-78.743* (42.626)
VER846	-3389.70*** (444.36)	-3356.40*** (448.36)	-3427.40*** (439.00)

	Full Model	Alternative Model	Unconstrained Model
Dependent	SER: 90.95	SER: 91.67	SER: 91.40
Variable: P2	DW: 2.1779	DW: 2.0371	DW: 2.0888
Independent Variables:			
CONSTANT	6407.80***	6311.70***	6294.50***
	(482.64)	(465.22)	(466.84)
QD1	-0.001044***	-0.0010518***	-0.001033***
	(0.0002938)	(0.0002829)	(0.0002837)
QD2	0.0002582	0.0001992	0.0002009
	(0.0001646)	(0.00015849)	(0.00015886)
QD3	-0.0006137***	-0.0006137***	-0.0005744**
	(0.0000817)	(0.00007824)	(0.00007845)
QD3814	-0.0007131***	-0.0006863***	-0.0007143**
	(0.0001682)	(0.0001591)	(0.0001592)
YD82	0.61497**	0.5718**	0.6102**
	(0.23607)	(0.22779)	(0.22843)
GAS82	-6.9261***	-5.4381**	-5.69**
	(2.2096)	(2.1254)	(2.1364)
OPEC2	2.7063***	2.5135***	2.4618***
	(0.81553)	(0.784)	(0.7906)
CSICH(-1)	638.71***	480.71**	504.38***
	(195.39)	(186.25)	(186.17)
DUM3	-194.76***	-184.23***	-186.41***
	(28.506)	(27.609)	(27.632)
DUM74	778.90***	822.55***	805.19***
	(47.356)	(45.713)	(45.781)
VER814	1007.90***	993.07***	1006.90***
	(144.14)	(136.12)	(136.21)
VER846	206.01**	238.78***	220.20***
	(81.305)	(78.169)	(78.303)

	Full Model	Alternative Model	Unconstrained Model
Dependent	SER: 161.55	SER: 156.30	SER: 159.56
Variable: P3	DW: 1.6632	DW: 1.8245	DW: 1.9117
Independent Variables:			
CONSTANT	10203.00***	10460.00***	10795.00***
	(693.40)	(688.33)	(698.53)
QD1	-0.0003714	-0.0002471	-0.0002173
	(0.00042)	(0.0004094)	(0.0004012)
QD1846	0.002135***	0.002178***	0.002168***
	(0.0002467)	(0.0002416)	(0.0002478)
QD2	-0.0008845***	-0.0007911***	-0.0008748**
	(0.0002434)	(0.000236)	(0.0002307)
QD3	-0.0005595***	-0.00055302***	-0.0005914**
	(0.0001217)	(0.000117)	(0.0001165)
QD3814	0.0009598***	0.0009589***	0.0009319**
	(0.00009034)	(0.00008986)	(0.00009144)
YD82	1.1158***	1.041***	0.9799***
	(0.34196)	(0.34057)	(0.3417)
GAS82	-21.815***	-24.137***	-25.748***
	(3.3946)	(3.2957)	(3.4302)
OPEC2	5.0151***	5.7213***	6.2435***
	(1.1773)	(1.1208)	(1.1748)
CSICH(-2)	693.75**	636.14**	578.84**
	(281.46)	(270.43)	(264.68)
DUM3	-287.07***	-260.27***	-246.25***
	(41.899)	(41.176)	(41.02)
DUM74	583.71***	518.66***	536.68***
	(70.691)	(67.369)	(67.873)

	Full Model	Alternative Model	Unconstrained Model
Dependent Variable: QD1	SER: 20062.90 DW: 1.8822	SER: 19948.60 DW: 1.7351	SER: 19463.30 DW: 1.6804
Independent Variables:			
CONSTANT	1648300.00*** (132290.00)	1676200.00*** (131220.00)	1665400.00*** (134420.00)
WS1	-180.12*** (17.674)	-172.38*** (17.722)	-119.30*** (19.495)
WS2	-39.118* (19.932)	---	---
WS3	97.022*** (17.031)	77.529*** (13.998)	67.639*** (14.494)
YD82	1203.80*** (64.647)	1169.80*** (65.393)	1031.40*** (68.931)
GAS82	1875.10*** (642.62)	1480.60** (588.03)	1512.40** (599.15)
OPEC2	-581.90*** (207.37)	-445.98** (193.61)	-257.68 (200.34)
UN(-4)	-16070.00*** (3429.9)	-18045.00*** (3181.2)	-14709.00*** (3297.10)
DUM4	-34959.00*** (9824.30)	-42644.00*** (9179.60)	-60316.00*** (9619.40)

(Quarterly VER dummy variables--not reported)

	Full Model	Alternative Model	Unconstrained Model
Dependent Variable: QD2	SER: 62289.20 DW: 2.3091	SER: 63268.50 DW: 2.3180	SER: 63167.00 DW: 2.3283
Independent Variables:			
CONSTANT	45725.00 (246670.00)	235980.00 (216170.00)	254010.00 (219030.00)
WS1	-29.495 (29.096)	-34.532 (33.007)	-39.80 (34.943)
WS2	58.683 (49.092)	---	---
W2814	-18.105 (108.19)	---	---
W2846	24.22 (130.56)	---	---
WS3	-37.02 (38.334)	-16.528 (22.761)	-14.621 (23.362)
W3814	-5.4684 (82.923)	-17.887*** (4.1206)	-17.885*** (4.1651)
W3846	25.513 (94.881)	-4.7467 (6.3173)	-4.1489 (6.3905)
YD82	407.71*** (110.03)	436.17*** (105.89)	433.88*** (108.98)
UNCH(-1)	-65343.00*** (16059.00)	-53985.00*** (14260.00)	-57925.00*** (14484.00)
CSICH(-3)	271670.00** (130530.00)	274860.00** (121930.00)	303250.00** (124450.00)
DUM1	181840.00*** (30374.00)	151710.00*** (27043.00)	169050.00*** (27678.00)

	Full Model	Alternative Model	Unconstrained Model
Dependent Variable: QD3	SER: 97502 DW: 2.1963	SER: 120210 DW: 1.5587	SER: 116470 DW: 1.6044
Independent Variables:			
CONSTANT	1834100.00* (1015200.00)	2597300.00*** (944700.00)	1470200.00 (1011900.00)
WS1	24.242 (23.934)	187.54*** (63.384)	76.004 (68.423)
WS2	-346.86*** (47.384)	---	---
W2814	-19.35* (10.958)	---	---
W2846	-47.566*** (14.482)	---	---
WS3	47.678 (48.400)	-266.38*** (39.221)	-201.95*** (43.449)
YD82	720.89 (430.52)	125.90 (430.52)	711.11 (439.94)
GAS82	-14796.00*** (2616.60)	-17401.00*** (2841.90)	-14779.00*** (3074.40)
OPEC2	1703.30** (832.38)	13633.40*** (914.82)	2787.30*** (979.94)
CSI(-1)	1034900.00*** (152440.00)	1057500.00*** (164990.00)	1035200.00*** (172900.00)
DUM2	163470.00*** (29959.00)	131030.00*** (30757.00)	141000.00*** (32320.00)
T	-3064.30 (6891.40)	-7163.00 (6132.10)	-12529.00* (6486.70)

	Full Model	Alternative Model	Unconstrained Model
Dependent	SER: 451.86	SER: 480.31	SER: 143.387
Variable: W1	DW: 0.4158	DW: 0.3910	DW: 1.4871
Independent Variables:			
CV310	0.88526***	1.0859***	---
	(0.21234)	(0.24766)	
CV311*VER814	-0.20244*	-0.18428	---
	(0.11630)	(0.14089)	
CV312*VER846	-0.53283***	-0.59655***	---
	(0.14377)	(0.16255)	
CONSTANT	---	---	-2053.70
			(1136.10)
JPMC/YDOL	---	---	0.02376
			(0.09249)
(JPMC/YDOL)*VER814	---	---	0.06573
			(0.3564)
(JPMC/YDOL)*VER846	---	---	-0.2475*
			(0.1252)
W3	---	---	0.1806*
			(0.09067)
W3814	---	---	0.07443
			(0.1161)
W3846	---	---	-0.3833**
			(0.1721)
S	---	---	1.2729
			(0.793)
YD82	---	---	3.1410***
			(0.4191)
GAS82	---	---	-4.651
			(4.1698)
OPEC2	---	---	-1.5206
			(1.2796)
UN(-4)	---	---	-21.523
			(20.973)
DUM4	---	---	161.9***
			(49.697)
VER814	---	---	-630.56
			(1543.1)
VER846	---	---	4392.3***
			(1362.9)

	Full Model	Alternative Model	Unconstrained Model
Dependent	SER: 471.60	SER: 367.28	SER: 217.607
Variable: W3	DW: 0.2071	DW: 1.3112	DW: 1.3829
Independent Variables:			
CV130	---	-1.4320 (0.85549)	---
CV131*VER814	---	1.2115** (0.59683)	---
CV132*VER846	---	1.1176* (0.56434)	---
CONSTANT	---	---	6226.10** (2617.50)
USLMC*VER846	---	---	0.893** (0.3333)
W1	---	---	0.06617 (0.1679)
W1814	---	---	0.3266 (0.2302)
W1846	---	---	-0.07369 (0.4173)
S	---	---	4.1309*** (1.2621)
YD82	---	---	-0.5983 (1.265)
GAS82	---	---	-24.786*** (7.189)
OPEC2	---	---	7.671*** (2.1678)
UNCH(-1)	---	---	79.397 (81.493)
CSI(-1)	---	---	-459.13 (575.55)
CSICH(-3)	---	---	315.96 (494.30)
T	---	---	17.887 (20.424)
DUM2	---	---	-119.86 (139.62)
VER814	---	---	-1537.60 (1478.50)
VER846	---	---	1494.80 (3071.00)

Appendix IV: VER's Effects on Consumer Surplus and on National Welfare

Although this thesis does not focus on the VER's impact on domestic consumers, yet an approximation of these effects can be calculated by using the model's slope coefficients and predicted changes in quantities. For example, consumer surplus (CS) is defined as the measure of the difference between the amount consumers are willing to pay for goods and the amount they actually pay for those goods. Formally,

$$CS = \int_0^{QD} P(X) \, dX - P*QD \tag{18}$$

where $P(X)$ is the inverse demand curve, P is the transaction price and Q is quantities sold. Substituting the inverse demand equation in (11a) into (18) and simplifying terms yield

$$CS_i = -(\hat{b}_{ii} * QD^2_i)/2$$

where $\hat{b}_{ii}$ is the estimated coefficient on own quantity and QD_i is the actual quantity of Japanese, U.S. small or U.S. large cars purchased in a given period.

Assessment of the VER's effect on consumer welfare requires estimation of the change in CS which occurred during the VER period. The change in CS is therefore

$$\Delta CS_i = [-(\hat{b}_{ii} * QD^2_i) + (\hat{b}_{ii} * \hat{QD}^2_i)]/2$$

where $\hat{b}_{ii}$ is the slope with the VER, $\hat{b}_{ii}$ is the slope without the VER, QD_i are actual quantities demanded and $\hat{QD}_i$ are predicted quantities demanded without the VER. The validity of this formula for calculating the change in consumer welfare is contingent upon the assumption of a downward sloping demand curve. However, in cases where the demand curve is upward sloping (as is the case where the transitional inverse demand curves for U.S. large cars in the early VER period and for Japanese cars in the late VER period have positive slope coefficients on own quantities), adequate assessment of the VER's consumer welfare effects is precluded. Therefore, the change in CS is approximated by assuming that $\hat{b}_{ii}$ is the same with or without the VER. This assumption implies that the estimated change in CS reflects the VER's effects in the neighborhood of the pre-VER equilibrium. A summary of the VER's effects on the welfare of domestic consumers (denominated in 1982 dollars) is presented below in Table A4.1.[93]

As expected, domestic consumers suffered a reduction in welfare through the imposition of the VER. Over the entire VER period, consumer surplus was reduced by approximately $5.7 billion. The cost of the VER to domestic consumers of Japanese cars was approximately $3.2 billion, while the cost to domestic consumers of U.S. large cars was approximately $2.5 billion. During the late VER period--the period when the incidence of the VER was higher--the cost to consumers was greater.

However, the estimated gains by U.S. manufacturers and domestic dealers outweigh the losses incurred by domestic automobile purchasers. Overall, national welfare increased by $6.5 billion. The VER generated profits for members of the domestic automobile industry (including dealers) of $12.24 billion, while consumer losses were approximately $5.7 billion. If consumer losses are indeed overstated because benefits from quality enhancement are not taken into account, the increase in national welfare which accompanied the VER is even greater.

---

[93]For U.S. small cars, the estimated slope coefficients on own quantities were not significantly different from zero. Thus, the change in CS was not calculated for consumers of U.S. small cars. Since the transaction prices were not adjusted for changes in product quality which accompanied the VER, the negative impact of the VER on consumers is overstated by these estimates. Ostensibly, increases in prices and limited availability of cars is a cost to consumers, while quality enhancement is a benefit. Not all increments to quality can be considered a benefit, however, since some options placed on cars by the manufacturers are not desired by consumers.

Table A4.1: VER's Effects on Welfare of U.S. Consumers

	Early VER Period	Late VER Period	Full VER Period
Japanese Cars	-0.91	-2.29	-3.20
U.S. Large Cars	-0.53	-1.88	-2.41

References

Adams, Walter, ed. (1986), *The Structure of American Industry*, MacMillan Publishing Company, New York, 7th ed.

Aizcorbe, Ana M. (1986), *The Competitiveness of U.S. Automobile Firms: A Neoclassical Cost Function Estimation of the Production Costs of U.S. and Japanese Firms*, Ph.D. dissertation, Boston College.

------, Clifford Winston and Ann Friedlaender (1987), "Cost Competitiveness of the U.S. Automobile Industry," in Clifford Winston and Associates, *Blind Intersection? Policy and the Automobile Industry*, The Brookings Institution, Washington, D.C., pp. 6-35.

Appelbaum, Elie (1982), "The Estimation of the Degree of Oligopoly Power," *Journal of Econometrics*, vol. 19, pp. 287-299.

Automotive News Market Data Book, various issues.

Baker, Jonathan B. and Timothy F. Bresnahan (1985), "The Gains from Merger or Collusion in Product-Differentiated Industries," in P.A. Geroski, L. Phlips and A. Ulph, eds., *Oligopoly, Competition and Welfare*, Basil Blackwell, Oxford, pp. 59-76.

Barten, A.P. (1969), "Maximum Likelihood Estimation of a Complete System of Demand Equations," *European Economic Review*, vol. 1, pp. 7-73.

Bowley, Arthur L. (1924), *The Mathematical Groundwork of Economics*, Oxford University Press.

Bresnahan, Timothy F. (1981), "Departures From Marginal Cost-Pricing in the American Automobile Industry," *Journal of Econometrics*, vol. 17, pp. 201-227.

------ (1982), "The Oligopoly Solution Concept is Identified," *Economics Letters*, vol. 10, pp. 87-92.

------ (June 1987), "Competition and Collusion in the American Automobile Industry: The 1955 Price War," *Journal of Industrial Economics*, vol. 35 (June), no. 4, pp. 457-482.

------ (1989), "Empirical Studies of Industries With Market Power," in R. Schmalensee and R.D. Willig, eds., *Handbook of Industrial Organization*, vol. 2, pp. 1011-1057.

------ and Peter C. Reiss (1985), "Dealer and Manufacturer Margins," *Rand Journal of Economics*, vol. 16 (Summer), no. 2, pp. 253-268.

Caves, Richard (1987), *American Industry: Structure, Conduct, Performance*, 6th ed., Prentice-Hall, Inc., New Jersey.

Charles River Associates (1976), *Impact of Trade Policies on the U.S. Automobile Market*, prepared for Bureau of International Labor Affairs, U.S. Department of Labor, Charles River Associates, Cambridge.

Chow, G. (1957), *Demand for Automobiles in the U.S.: A Study in Consumer Durables*, North-Holland, Amsterdam.

Collyns, Charles and Steven Dunaway (1987), "The Cost of Trade Restraints: The Case of Japanese Automobile Exports to the United States," *International Monetary Fund Staff Papers*, (March), pp. 150-175.

Crandall, Robert W. (1984), "Import Quotas and the Automobile Industry: The Costs of Protectionism," in U.S. Congress, Committee on Foreign Relations, *Free Trade--Myth or Reality*, pp. 82-109.

------ (1985), "Assessing the Impacts of the Automobile Voluntary Export Restraints upon U.S. Automobile Prices," paper delivered at the Society of Government Economists (December).

Cubbin, John (1975), "Quality Change and Pricing Behaviour in the United Kingdom Car Industry 1956-1968," *Economica*, vol. 42, pp. 43-58.

Data Resources, Inc., "Using the DRI North American Light Vehicle Model On-Line," May 1983.

Deaton, Angus and John Muellbauer (1980a), *Economics and Consumer Behavior*, Cambridge University Press, Cambridge.

------ and ------ (1980b), "An Almost Ideal Demand System," *American Economic Review*, vol. 70 (June), no. 3.

de Wolff, P. (1938), "The Demand for Passenger Cars in the United States," *Econometrica*, vol. 6 (April), pp. 113-129.

Dinopoulos, Elias and Mordechai E. Kreinin (1988), "Effects of the U.S.-Japan Auto VER on European Prices and on U.S. Welfare," *Review of Economics and Statistics*, pp. 484-491.

Dixit, Avinash (1986), "Optimal Trade and Industrial Policies for the U.S. Automobile Industry," in Robert Feenstra, ed., *Empirical Methods for International Trade*, MIT press, Cambridge, MA.

Edmunds New Car Prices, various issues.

Feenstra, Robert C. (1984), "Voluntary Export Restraint in U.S. Autos, 1980-81: Quality, Employment, and Welfare Effects," in Robert Baldwin and Anne Krueger, eds., *The Structure and Evolution of Recent U.S. Trade Policy*, University of Chicago Press, Chicago, Il., pp. 35-59.

------ (1985), "Automobile Prices and Protection: The U.S.-Japan Trade Restraint," *Journal of Policy Modeling*, vol. 7, pp. 49-68.

Fellner, William (1965), *Competition Among the Few: Oligopoly and Similar Market Structures*, Augustus M. Kelley, New York.

Friedman, James (1987), *Oligopoly Theory*, Cambridge University Press, Cambridge.

Gelfand, Matthew D. and Pablo T. Spiller (1987), "Entry Barriers and Multiproduct Oligopolies: Do they Forebear or Spoil?" *International Journal of Industrial Organization*, vol. 5, pp. 101-113.

Geroski, P.A., L. Phlips and A. Ulph (1985), *Oligopoly, Competition and Welfare*, Basil Blackwell, Oxford, pp. 1-18.

Gollop, Frank M. and Mark J. Roberts (1979), "Firm Interdependence in Oligopolistic Markets," *Journal of Econometrics*, vol. 10, pp. 313-331.

Golomb, D., M. Luckey, J. Saalberg, B. Richardson and K. Joscelyn (1979), *Wharton Econometrics Forecasting Associates: An Analysis of Wharton EFA Automobile Demand Model*, UMI Research Press, Ann Arbor Michigan.

Gomez-Ibanez, Jose A., Robert A. Leone, and Stephen A. O'Connell (1983), "Restraining Auto Imports: Does Anyone Win?" *Journal of Policy Analysis and Management*, vol. 2, no. 2, pp. 196-219.

Greenhut, M.L. and H. Ohta (1979), "Vertical Integration of Successive Oligopolies," *American Economic Review*, (March), pp. 137-141.

Gujarati, Damodar N. (1988), *Basic Econometrics*, 2nd ed., McGraw-Hill Book Co., New York.

Guide to the Motor Industry of Japan, 1982.

Hamburger, Michael J. (1967), "Interest Rates and the Demand for Consumer Durable Goods," *American Economic Review*, vol. 57 (December), pp. 1131-1153.

Harris, Richard (1984), "Why Voluntary Export Restraints are 'Voluntary'," *Canadian Journal of Economics*, vol. 18, pp. 799-809.

Hickok, Susan (1985), "The Consumer Cost of U.S. Trade Restraints," *Quarterly Review*, Federal Reserve Bank of New York, vol. 10 (Summer), no. 2, pp. 1-12.

Houthakker, H.S. and L.D. Taylor (1966), *Consumer Demand in the United States, 1929-70: Analysis and Projections*, Harvard University Press, Cambridge, MA.

Hunker, Jeffrey Allen (1983), *Structural Change in the U.S. Automobile Industry*, Lexington Books, Lexington, MA.

Hymans, Saul H. (1970), "Consumer Durable Spending: Explanation and Prediction," in A.M. Okun and G.L. Perry, eds., *Brookings Papers on Economic Activity*, vol. 2, pp. 173-199.

Itoh, Motoshige and Yoshiyasu Ono (1984), "Tariffs vs. Quotas Under Duopoly of Heterogeneous Goods," *Journal of International Economics*, vol. 17, pp. 359-373.

Iwata, Gyoichi (1974), "Measurement of Conjectural Variations in Oligopoly," *Econometrica*, vol. 42, no. 5, pp. 947-966.

J.D. Power and Associates (1981-1986), *Customer Satisfaction Indices*.

Juster, Thomas and Paul Wachtel (1972), "Anticipatory and Objective Models of Durable Goods Demand," *American Economic Review*, vol. 62, pp. 564-579.

Krishna, Kala (1983), "Trade Restrictions and Facilitating Practices," dissertation paper, Princeton University.

------ (1984/89), "Trade Restrictions and Facilitating Practices," *Harvard Institute of Economic Research*, discussion paper, no. 1119, (December); *Journal of International Economics*, vol. 26, nos. 3/4, (May 1989), pp. 251-70.

------ (1987), "What do VERS Do?" *Harvard Institute of Economic Research*, discussion paper, no. 1323, (June).

Kwoka, John E., Jr. (1984), "Market Power and market Change in the U.S. Automobile Industry," *Journal of Industrial Economics*, vol. 32, no. 4, pp. 509-522.

Liang, J. (1988), "Price Reaction Functions and Conjectural Variations: An Application to the Breakfast Cereal Industry," research paper, Board of Governors of the Federal Reserve System.

Mannering, Fred and Clifford Winston (1985), "A Dynamic Empirical Analysis of Household Vehicle Ownership and Utilization," *Rand Journal of Economics*, vol. 16, no. 2, pp. 215-236.

------ and ------ (1987), "Economic Effects of Voluntary Export Restraints," in Clifford Winston and Associates, *Blind Intersection? Policy and the Automobile Industry*, The Brookings Institution, Washington, D.C., pp. 61-67.

Motor Vehicle Manufacturers Association of the United States, Inc. (1986), *MVMA Motor Vehicle Facts & Figures*.

National Automobile Dealers Association (1987), *NADA Data for 1987*.

Nihon Keizai Shimbun, Inc., Nikkei Telecom Japan News and Retrieval, data base.

Ono, Yoshiyasu (1982), "Price Leadership: A Theoretical Analysis," *Economica*, vol. 49 (February), pp. 11-20.

------ (1984), "Profitability of Export Restraint," *Journal of International Economics*, vol. 16, pp. 335-343.

Pashigian, Bedros Peter (1965), *The Distribution of Automobiles, An Economic Analysis of the Franchise System*, Prentice-Hall, Inc., Englewood Cliffs, N.J.

Pollack, Robert (1983), "The Treatment of 'Quality' in the Cost of Living Index," *Journal of Public Economics*, vol. 20, pp. 25-53.

Richardson, Barbara C., Lawrence D. Segel, W. Steven Barnett and Kent B. Joscelyn (1979, 1980 and 1982), *An Inventory of Selected Mathematical Models Relating to the Motor Vehicle Transportation System and Associated Literature*, vols. 1-3, Michigan.

Rousslang, Donald and Stephen Parker (1984), "Cross-Price Elasticities of U.S. Import Demand," *Review of Economics and Statistics*, (August) p. 521.

Schmalensee, R. and J.F. Thisse (1986), "Perceptual Maps and the Optimal Location of New Products," Center of Operations Research and Econometric Core Reprint 8620.

Shaked, Avner and John Sutton (1982), "Natural Oligopolies and International Trade: An Introduction," International Centre for Economics and Related Disciplines (ICERD) Discussion Paper no. 50, London School of Economics.

Stein, Martin M. and Marianne Beauregard (1984), "Auto Plan: A Simplified Automotive Forecasting Model," working paper, Abt Associates Inc., Cambridge.

Stone, J.R.N. (1954), "Linear Expenditure Systems and Demand Analysis: An Application to the Pattern of British Demand," *Economic Journal*, vol. 64, pp. 511-527.

Suits, Daniel B. (1961), "Exploring Alternative Formulations of Automobile Demand," *Review of Economics and Statistics*, pp. 66-69.

Tarr, D. and M. Morkre (1984), "Aggregate Cost to the U.S. of Tariffs and Quotas on Imports," *Federal Trade Commission, Bureau of Economics Staff Report*.

Tishler, Asher (1982), "The Demand for Cars and the Price of Gasoline: The User Cost Approach," *Review of Economics and Statistics*, pp. 184-190.

Toder, Eric J. (1978), *Trade Policy and the U.S. Automotive Industry*, Charles River Associates Research Report, Praeger Publishers, New York.

Train, Kenneth (1986), *Qualitative Choice Analysis: Theory, Econometrics, and an Application to Automobile Demand*, MIT Press, Cambridge.

Tsurumi, Hiroki and Yoshi Tsurumi (1983), "U.S.-Japan Automobile Trade," *Journal of Econometrics*, vol. 23, pp. 193-210.

U.S. Department of Labor, Bureau of Labor Statistics, *Employment Hours and Earnings*, various issues.

U.S. Department of Transportation (1980), *The U.S. Automotive Industry*.

United States, Congress, Joint Economic Committee (1980), *U.S. Trade and Investment Policy: Imports and the future of the American Automobile Industry*, hearing before the Joint Economic Committee, Congress of the United States, Ninety-Sixth Congress, second session, (March).

United States, Congress, House, Committee on Ways and Means, Subcommittee on Trade (1985), *Japanese Voluntary Restraints on Auto Exports to the United States*, hearings before the Subcommittee on Trade of the Committee on Ways and Means, House of Representatives, Ninety-Ninth Congress, first session, (February and March).

Varian, Hal R. (1978), *Microeconomic Analysis*, W.W. Norton & Company, New York.

Wards Automotive Yearbook, various issues.

Westin, R.B. (1975), "Empirical Implications of Infrequent Purchase Behavior in a Stock-Adjustment Model," *American Economic Review*, vol. 65, pp. 384-396.

Wharton Econometric Forecasting Associates, Inc. (1977), "An Analysis of the Automobile Market: Modeling the Long-Run Determinants of the Demand for Automobiles," vols. 1, 2 and 3, prepared for the U.S. Department of Transportation, Transportation Systems Center, Cambridge, M.A.

White, Lawrence J., (1971), *The Automobile Industry Since 1945*, Harvard University Press, Cambridge, Massachusetts.

Willig, Robert D. and Mark A. Dutz (1987), "U.S.-Japanese VER: A Case Study from a Competition Policy Perspective" in Organization for Economic Co-operation and Development, *The Cost of Restricting Imports: The Automobile Industry*, OECD, Paris.

Yoffie, David (1983), *Power and Protectionism: Strategies of the Newly Industrializing Countries*, New York: Columbia University Press.

Index

For Product Safety Concerns and Information please contact our EU representative GPSR@taylorandfrancis.com Taylor & Francis Verlag GmbH, Kaufingerstraße 24, 80331 München, Germany

Printed and bound by CPI Group (UK) Ltd, Croydon, CR0 4YY

08/05/2025

01864494-0004